SINS OF COMMISSION

SINS OF COMMISSION

WILLIAM
DOUGLAS HOME

MICHAEL RUSSELL

First published in Great Britain 1985
by Michael Russell (Publishing) Ltd
The Chantry, Wilton, Salisbury, Wiltshire
Set in Pilgrim by The Spartan Press Ltd, Lymington
Printed and bound in Great Britain
by Biddles Ltd, Guildford and King's Lynn

ISBN 0 85955 115 6

Contents

The Reluctant Soldier

When my mother died, my sister Bridget sent me all the letters I had written to my parents during the Second World War. It came as a surprise to me that they existed still.

Re-reading them, it seemed to me that, covering the period they do, they might be of some interest to those who find war and its effect on individuals a worthwhile study. And of interest, too, to those who are opposed to war in any form and seek exemption from it on religious grounds. Also to those who, recognising that in certain circumstances wars must be fought, seek to change the policy adopted by their government in order to provide some opportunity for shortening the conflict.

To the second category I belonged instinctively – though not in practice, since I knew my limitations. Therefore I found refuge in the third, believing that the war aims (or lack of them) of the Churchill government, effectively and tragically, denied the opportunity of overthrowing Hitler to all those in Germany who (in uniform or out of it) secretly opposed him.

What I sought was some constructive war aim which would help the dissidents point out to the German people that, should they give their support, an honourable peace could be negotiated by a government that had abandoned Nazism. As it was, of course, the policy of unconditional surrender covered everybody, pro- or anti- Hitler, while the later declaration that the terms of the Atlantic Charter did not cover Germany were equally destructive to the chances of the anti-Nazis bringing off a *coup d'état*, (though in 1944 they tried it, too late, in the July Plot).

These matters were what exercised my mind throughout the war and are reflected in these letters, which are sometimes pretentious, frequently hurried, occasionally bitter and intermittently, I'm afraid, facetious. Never mind, they are a true reflection of my feelings at the time.

I am well aware that there are those who deplore on principle a story such as mine, because they reject the whole idea of a soldier, even a reluctant one, questioning, under any circumstances, any aspect of the policy adopted by a wartime coalition, let alone an order given to him in the field. For them, I have no message – only a suggestion that they should bear in mind that even some of the professionals in Hitler's army felt it necessary, in 1944, to reason why.

But there are others, including many servicemen, who know that in this age of conscript armies loyalties are sometimes strained and pressures put on individuals unsuited to the task allotted to them. They accept, as do the first group, that a soldier who has volunteered to be a regular is duty bound – unless his country is in danger from the very people from whom he takes his orders – to do what his superiors require of him. At the same time they can understand, unlike the first group, that the pressure on a conscript may prove to be unacceptable. For them, my message is that they are on to something.

And to all those younger readers who are now of much the same age as I was then, my message is – consider yourselves lucky you are not in the same boat; and ask yourselves what action (or inaction) you would contemplate in such a situation. And, maybe, write and tell me.

The first letters, written during the last months of 1939, could not have come as a surprise to either of my parents. They both knew that, for some years, I had been wondering what I would do, assuming that the crunch came. They were well aware of all the letters I had written to the press – most notably the *Scotsman* – during the prewar years. They were clear about my view (shared by my father) that the Versailles Treaty had done nothing to avert a second world war by its unimaginative treatment of the losers of the first, and they had heard me holding forth about a new approach to foreign policy. This was to involve the internationalisation of strategic points and the abandonment of that old stance of dubious morality that anybody who already had one was entitled to an empire, but not anybody who wished to emulate the good example.

They listened patiently to all my calls for international cooperation founded on a universal law, which did not exist then and, alas, does not exist yet. And, after Munich, they were often treated to a lecture from me on the need for what is now known as a summit meeting between all the great powers – to initiate the new approach to foreign policy I called for in my innocence. Finally, when war broke out, they noted that I did not leap to join the colours. Yes, they must have been prepared for stormy weather.

All my friends were joining up; Brian Johnston, with whom I shared digs in South Eaton Place, was in the Grenadiers. I joined the Fire Service for a short time but left it to become a member of a journalistic group. I went fact-finding with its editor on tours abroad. One morning in Rome we had taxied to the airport to get on the plane for Venice, en route for Sofia. On the tarmac stood a German plane with a swastika on its side. We boarded it because our tickets, bought in London from Imperial Airways, indicated that, indeed, this was the plane on which we were booked. After take-off, down the gangway came a limping German pilot. He stopped by our seats and turned a lever near the ceiling. I said to my editor, 'He's opening a trap door and he's going to drop us out.' 'No,' the pilot replied, in perfect English, 'I'm closing off the ventilation. It's cold over the mountains.' On that two-hour journey, during which we wave-hopped in the later stages of the Adriatic, I thought to myself that if we could travel in a German plane, during a war, with tickets bought in London, no doubt paid for in some manner to the German airline, surely international cooperation could be nurtured on a larger scale to the advantage of all.

I came back to England and sat down and wrote a letter to my parents.

35 South Eaton Place,
London SW1

Dear Pa and Ma,

I hope you don't mind, but I registered as an objector on Sat: I saw no alternative. I asked if I could be registered for non-combatant duties, and they said 'Not unless you register as a C.O.' So I did.

One day I shall have to appear before a tribunal. I trust it doesn't upset you too much. I'm not really a conscientious objector, as I pointed out in the form I had to fill in. I have no reason to suppose that I wouldn't steal, commit adultery, or kill anybody when I thought it the only thing to do or when I was too weak to resist it. But with regard to this war, I *cannot* see that it's necessary; peace by negotiation is always possible. If these gentlemen suggested it, and it was turned down, then I might reconsider my position; but they haven't and they won't except on preconceived terms – which is worse than not doing it at all.

The question for the tribunal is not whether I'm a conscientious objector but whether I'm to be forced to kill people who, in my view, have had a raw deal.

I'm not shaken by the reported behaviour of the German troops. The thing that matters is not what people do, but why they do it.

There are three alternatives: (1) to win this war and beat Germany, (2) for them to win and beat us, (3) to compromise.

As the Italian Ambassador remarked, the first two would be equally tragic. In the case of (1) we're not in a position to rule Europe; in the case of (2) it wouldn't be nice for Germany to rule the world. Therefore (3) is the only one.

Hope you don't mind that decision. Most of my friends have dropped me now, except the only ones I really like.

Love,
WILLIAM

That letter indicates, with clarity, the views I held at that time, the confusion in my mind about what attitude I should adopt, the doubts that plagued me as to whether or not I was qualified to register as an objector. It drew an immediate response from my mother.

35 South Eaton Place

My dear Ma,

Thanks very much for your letter. Although I am 99% a conscientious objector as far as killing people goes, I cannot swear that I wouldn't kill an individual in self-defence. It's therefore impossible to call myself entirely genuine. My own opinion is that it's perfectly possible to be a C.O. as far as wars go, refusing to kill *innocent* people on the other side, but evidently that is not the view held by the tribunals.

The only other thing is whether you can be an objector because you are convinced politically that you've no right to be killing people in this war because you've no right to be in the war at all. I should have thought that was O.K., but again you tell me that is not the opinion of the tribunals.

If that is absolutely certain, then it's no use appearing before them except for the personal satisfaction of sticking up for one's principles, which I should like to do. I have a slight feeling that people may say I hadn't the courage to stick up for it in public – though I don't really mind what people say. And if it's only going to get a little publicity and cause acute embarrassment and *fail in its purpose* (which fact I'm accepting as true from you!), then it's not worth doing.

I've therefore written to the Labour people asking them to remove my name, at the same time pointing out that it's not because I've changed my mind, that I still think this war's a crime, and that peace by negotiation now is the only possible solution. Between the alternatives of obeying the State or jail, I choose the former because the day may come when obedience to the State will be the only safeguard against anarchy.

Presumably they'll place me on the military register now. I don't much mind, in fact it should be a great relief. I don't suppose I'm constructed strongly enough to become a martyr to any cause. I also suppose that one has salved one's conscience by holding out against the thing as long as one can, until – as in Germany – one has to do it. And then people expect the Germans to revolt against Hitler. Blimey!

I'm not worried about minesweepers or ambulances. The whole thing's a war effort and it's no use splitting straws, and if one's going to military service one may as well do it as scheduled by the Government. I haven't the least intention of volunteering for anything, because one of my basic beliefs is that the best way to stop all wars is for individuals in every country to be as reluctant to fight in them as possible. Then the responsibility for them will be focused more and more on governments, on which of course it rests.

I trust you're all O.K. Judging by the wireless Churchill seems to be trying to start a revolution in France as a prelude to starving them to death in the blockade: he's bound to fail.

I give the war about a month more, if that. Still I've done that before.

Love,
WILLIAM

The optimistic note struck in the final sentence of that letter soon gave way to undiluted gloom, although in my next letter I was clearly clinging to the hope that I could stand for Parliament before my call-up papers came, not knowing at that time that one could do so even after one had been conscripted. This, to my delight, I learned much later.

35 South Eaton Place

Dear Dadda and Mamma,

Thanks very much for letters. I suppose I'll have to register, though I want to stand as a 'peace by negotiation' candidate before I'm called up. The awful thing is that even if Roosevelt, Mussolini, France and Germany all agreed to have a conference now or at any time in the future, the chances are that Churchill would refuse to have one. The war's got to end in 'peace by negotiation' one day, so the sooner the better.

There are still a few M.P.s, notably one Dick Stokes, who stick to their principles. Most of them are a hopeless set of sheep, however – and that goes for Lord Dunglass![1]

If we lose the war the situation's hopeless and if we win it, we or the French will do *exactly* the same as we did after the last one, thus ensuring another one in twenty-five years. The obvious alternative is neither to win nor lose – i.e. compromise.

I can't think how a lot of hopeless old politicians who have let things go to pot for twenty years have the effrontery to stand up and ask every young man in England to go and die in Belgium, so that they can repeat their imbecilities again. If one's thinking of the future, it's just as frightening to think of winning this war as of losing it. No two politicians have the same idea about what they'll go and do when they've won it – no Frenchman and Englishman can ever agree on that score anyhow.

There's only one chance of an intelligent future, and that is if Roosevelt and Mussolini can control themselves and Germany and us sufficiently to call a conference. It seems almost too late, but if Mussolini can be stopped coming in it might be possible. But then, as I say, Churchill has to be reckoned with.

With the possible exception of Chamberlain, there is nothing like an English politician for sending a whole battalion to be slaughtered with a gay, muddled irresponsibility.

However, it's no use pointing out these regrettable facts because there's nothing to be done about it. I don't quite know what I'm going to do. I may retire into the country to write my new play, or I may act at Brighton in my own, or I may join Victor Cazalet's anti-aircraft battalion to save being conscripted. He knows I'm a 99% pacifist, and is

[1] Alec, my eldest brother.

therefore not too keen on having me. However, he could if I wanted to join.

Which would you suggest?

Love,
WILLIAM

The summer months of 1940 dragged on. I continued with my playwrighting. Then in July I went to Windsor to act in a Noël Coward play called *The Young Idea*. The run concluded, I returned to London. On the mat, inside the front door, lay my call-up papers. Hence the theme of my next letter, written from a regimental camp near Maidenhead.

Maidenhead
Sunday

Dear Pa and Ma,

I feel as though I'd been here for twenty years. Inoculated yesterday – sleeping in tents – learning to salute tomorrow. The officer seems interested about my Certificate A, though when he sees me on the parade ground his interest will turn to amazement. We're all over our inoculation quite quickly, although I felt pretty queer last night. I don't know when we'll be let out into the town; I should think in a few days, but I don't think we ever get any leave. Still, I shall go and call on Lady Astor and an actor called James Mason who lives in Maidenhead. They say we train here for three months. Apart from the boredom which will be acute, it's not too bad, though I wouldn't give the food to Crisp.[1]

Love,
WILLIAM
('Bill' to the boys in my tent)

Dear Dadda and Mamma,

I was getting off this weekend, but now I'm on guard. It makes me sick. It's all due to the fact that I'm a lance corporal

[1] The landlord of my digs in London.

now, and so I have much more work to do. They had to make me one, as I'm going up for a commission.

I suppose the Guards thing is alright. It means staying here till November which doesn't cheer me up much. Thanks for letters.

If anyone feels like giving me a delayed birthday present I could do with a wrist watch (luminous) – one of those ones that shut up if possible, or with a guard. I'm only suggesting!

Love,

WILLIAM

The second paragraph of that last letter shows that the plot was beginning to thicken, with my promotion to lance corporal followed by selection as an October (1940) candidate. Acceptance of both indicates that I was following my earlier decision not to volunteer for anything, but only to accept what came my way. Although I'm bound to say that I was most surprised to learn that anybody should regard me as a suitable lance corporal, let alone an officer. The comment on the Guards was prompted by the fact that loyal but misguided friends had put me up as a Guards candidate. Some time elapsed before the call to OCTU came. During this period the regiment (the 7th Buffs) moved down to Kingsbridge, Devon, while I went on a course.

7th Batt. The Buffs,
c/o G.P.O. Antony,
Cornwall

Dear Dadda and Mamma,

Thanks very much for letters and money. We've moved again – at least I have because I'm on an N.C.O.s' course – to a place called Scraesdon Fort. It's not far from the other place. A gigantic spot, built to repel Napoleon, and it's just like being in the Foreign Legion. We sleep in the old stone vaults down hundreds of stairs and look out on the moat. People used to sleep in the dungeons, but rats like dogs hurried over them at night, so they moved them out before I got here.

There are miles of passages and dungeons and it's getting a bit chilly, but I'm well clothed.

The Regimental Sergeant Major told me not to walk with my hands behind my back this morning when I was strolling round the fort, which annoyed me a good deal. The officers here are quite efficient in instructing, but they take very little interest in the men, never by any chance speak to them, and are lacking in any sense of humour – including the Adjutant.

The Colonel might just force a smile if Hitler slipped on a banana skin in front of his office, but not much more. However, the sergeants are all right. I'm here for a month on this course, and then I suppose I go to my Company again and then to Sandhurst.

We had an invasion scare, or something, Sat. week. I expect you did too. It necessitated sitting in a ditch from 10 p.m. till 9 a.m. One officer fell 4 ft. into a ditch and the countryside was echoing with laughter, but otherwise nothing happened except for rumours. I spend my whole time imitating Churchill making a speech. Has the Hon. Edward moved yet? Thank Bridget for letters.

Love,
WILLIAM

The Hon. Edward referred to in that letter was (and still is) my younger brother, who had joined the Lanarkshire Yeomanry from Balliol. Perhaps a brief identification parade of my family might help the reader.

PA — My father, Lord Lieutenant of Berwickshire.

MA — My mother.

ALEC — My eldest brother, MP for South Lanark, later to spend most of the war in bed after an operation for spinal tuberculosis.

BRIDGET — My eldest sister, who worked in the children's hospital department which had moved into The Hirsel, my parents' home, for the duration.

HENRY My second brother, crippled by a riding accident before the war and on the staff of Scottish Command in Edinburgh.

RACHEL My second sister, wife of Billy Scott, MP for Roxburgh and Selkirk.

EDWARD Then a subaltern in the Lanarkshire Yeomanry, later to move to the Far East and be captured by the Japanese.

GEORGE My youngest brother, who joined the Air Force straight from school and went missing in 1942 from an aircraft on a training flight out of Vancouver Island.

By now the summons to the OCTU had arrived.

Royal Military College,
Camberley,
Surrey

Dear Dadda and Mamma,

Thanks for letters. I'm on a twenty-four-hour guard now, and found it a trifle chilly about 3 a.m. this morning. However my cold has practically gone.

It doesn't look as though we'll be getting any Christmas leave, but they might slip it in at the last minute. I doubt if it'd be more than a day or two.

The Colonel of the Grenadiers is coming down on Tuesday, so if I trip up and fall flat on my face when I'm saluting him, he'll probably refuse to have me.

Love,
WILLIAM

Royal Military College,
Camberley,
Surrey
Dec. 9th [1940]

Dear Ma and Pa,

Thanks very much for letters. Nothing much to report from

here. They tell me a large bomb fell at Eton, but I haven't been over to see George lately, as Johnston's car hasn't arrived.

Had dinner with Jimmy Lane-Fox[1] last night. I've taken to playing squash quite a lot now, and when we're on fire picquet at night we live in the billiard room and play snooker most of the night.

We interviewed the Grenadier Colonel the other day. I'm still somewhat attached to the Buffs, but I daresay it's the best to have incompetent officers in the Guards because the N.C.O.s are good enough to outweigh them. I haven't told the Colonel that.

Love,
WILLIAM

Royal Military College,
Camberley,
Surrey
Jan. 2nd, 1941

Dear Pa and Ma,

Got back all right and hadn't been here two days before I forgot one roll call and had dirty buttons on my cap and got 8 days C.B. My platoon commander, one Gerald Micklem in the Grenadier Guards, seems to think I'm casual (and he may be right) and he thinks he can change that by constantly reporting me (and there, I fear, he's wrong).

I've now reached a definite decision re the Grenadier Guards and I wrote yesterday to the Adjutant at Birdcage Walk, telling him I thought I was quite unsuited to be a Guards officer – an opinion which I felt was shared by my platoon commander here. And even if it wasn't, I really do feel much happier out of them, because they do indulge in all the spit and polish which annoys me and which I couldn't seriously enforce in others. So it will now be the Buffs, or an

[1] A Sandhurst instructor and friend.

Intelligence unit in which is my friend Rupert Raw from the Scots Guards and one or two other delightful people. Far more in my line.

I believe it's unusual to turn down a possible commission in the Guards – and naturally it is an attitude of mind that they find hard to understand. But they'll be none the worse for that.

I went to Cliveden last Sunday and Lady Astor was in very good form indeed.

Love,
WILLIAM

Royal Military College,
Camberley,
Surrey

Dear Dadda and Mamma,

Had a nasty chill on the stomach yesterday, due to sweating at drill followed by weapon training lectures in an acute east wind. So thoughtful of the Army to arrange things in that order. The Company Commander inspected us on sick parade and told me to pull my chin in. I tried my best to be sick over his boots. If there's any difference between Potsdam and the Sandhurst point of view, I'd like to find it out quite soon.

It's quite enjoyable here now the first rush is over. Johnston came down to lunch the other day. He was on manoeuvres the other day and talking back by field telephone to the Intelligence Officer who's a friend of his. He was meant to be reporting 'machine guns forward' etc., etc., but at that moment a pack of hounds came past and he started giving a commentary like Howard Marshall, saying 'Here comes the fox, slipping along the hedge, it's a lovely day.' Suddenly a crisp voice at the other end said, 'Come along, Johnston, less fooling please.' The Company Commander had taken over the telephone. I doubt if there's a word of truth in it.

There appears to be an air raid every night. Sirens everywhere, but no aeroplanes so far. I have to sit on a roof a bit this afternoon as a fire fighter and again tonight. However we get off Saturday, Wednesday and Thursday afternoons if there's no air raid precautions stuff.

Tubby Clayton[1] preached a sermon this morning about the last war. I could see no difference between it and a lecture on tactics by a Company Commander.

There are some wonderful staff sergeants here in the Scots Guards.

Love,
WILLIAM

R. M. C. Sandhurst
(Excuse blots)

Dear Pa and Ma,

Thanks very much for letters. I'm delighted to be able to say that, in view of my letter asking to resign and the fact that I had a bad report from my Platoon Commander, I've been turned down by the Grenadiers. Jimmy Lane Fox is disgusted and so is Major H. Vernon, who is Chief Instructor and kindly remarked that he thought I would have been very good indeed. My Company Commander, Maj. Blundell, offered to suggest me as a candidate for his regiment, the Scots Guards. In fact they've been delightful.

However, as I want to go into this G.H.Q. Intelligence Unit, I must get a commission in a regt. which won't mind me being transferred at once. I therefore thought the Buffs might permit that, as I'm really in that anyway. If that turns out impossible, the Chief Instructor said he could pop me into the Household Cavalry. Anyway, I'll notify you of my progress.

I saw George yesterday and played football against some eleven – but he wasn't playing. Routh[2] tells me he's going into the Air Force, but as the war will be over long before then it doesn't much matter. Routh's had a half crown on it being over by June.

[1] Founder padre of Toc H and chaplain to King George VI.

[2] Brother George's Eton house master.

I saw a photograph of you in the paper electing a peer or two. Hoping you're all very well.

Love,
WILLIAM

R.M.C. Sandhurst,
Camberley
Feb 2nd [1941]

Dear Dadda and Mamma,

Thanks very much for letters.

We had the funeral of three of those people who were killed by the bomb today. Most depressing, the whole thing. It really makes one wonder whether any useful solution can be achieved by blowing people to pieces who've done nothing to deserve it. And if we insist on going on with the war until Germany is beaten and then occupying the country, I can't believe we'll be very welcome guests. However, as America and Russia are both interested in looking after themselves by sheltering behind us and Germany respectively, I see little hope of any unselfish action from them. Mr Churchill appears to be trying to look more and more like Bismarck every day in that ridiculous bus conductor's uniform.

Hoping you're very well.

Love,
WILLIAM

That sad letter was my last from Sandhurst. I had passed out from that establishment and been posted back to the 7th Buffs – much to the amusement of my old tent-companions still in the ranks.

7th Batt. The Buffs,
Kingsbridge

Dear Pa and Ma,

Thanks very much for letters. It's my day off today and it's raining like nothing on earth. I'm going to Torquay to see

Cyril Maude acting in *The School for Scandal* and then having dinner with him afterwards. While walking through a garden of an old house on the coast here, whom should I meet but Clemie Waring[1] who lives here. I had dinner with them the other night. It's the house where Tennyson wrote 'Crossing the Bar' and the bar here moans all night like he said in his poem.

Hoping you are keeping very well.

Love,
WILLIAM

The Buffs

Dear Pa and Ma,

Many thanks for letters. It's blowing very hard tonight and I've got to go out and look at the sentries, which I'm not looking forward to. Otherwise we've had good weather.

Cyril Maude was rather delightful and talked about Henry Irving as though he had stayed with him last weekend. His extracts from *The School for Scandal* were very good.

The Colonel's coming down to inspect my platoon tomorrow. I've sent the dirtiest ones out for the day. My Company Commander's livid with me because I've let him in for singing two songs at the concert (which he does very well). He went out in a lifeboat the other day on a trial run and I made the signaller send a message in Morse saying 'England expects every man to bring back his dinner'. He made me change the guard that evening instead of him.

The Hon. George must be back by now. Ask him what is (a) a bird with a sharp beak, black and about half as big again as a gr. crested grebe, which dives; and (b) a bird a bit bigger than a puffin, black and white, which also dives, and lies on the water flapping its wings.

Love,
WILLIAM

[1] An old lady who had lived in Berwickshire when wife of our MP.

The Buffs
[Kingsbridge]

Dear Pa and Ma,

We're in the middle of our War Weapons Week and spend all our time marching round the town. I had to go to a town near here yesterday and supervise their parade. The parson at the drumhead service was speaking with the microphone back to front, and I had to go out and turn it round before the populace!

It's amazing about Hess. I expect he's here with a peace plan and that Hitler warned him that he'd disown him otherwise nobody would listen. I think the war will be over very shortly. As I forecast to you months ago, all the neutral countries are uniting in passive defence and the moment's rapidly approaching when they'll say 'Thanks awfully for fighting for us, but please stop starving us now' and the answer's not very easy to supply.

I'm doing two Noël Coward sketches at the concert here on Wednesday with an actress called Margaret Radclyffe who used to be in London and is now a Wren at Dartmouth.

And we have a dance tonight, so we're fairly busy.

Love,
WILLIAM

The Buffs

Dear Pa and Ma,

Thanks very much for letters. Here are 16 coupons. I heard Reid[1] saying he had nowhere to go for his leave around Nov. 14th or so, and couldn't get in to any hotels. So I told him you were always telling me to tell him to drop in at Hirsel. He said it'd be delightful if you really didn't mind and if Mrs Reid wouldn't be too frightened to go!

Would it be O.K? If so you might write to him and suggest it. He had all his clothes destroyed in Canterbury so he looks like a tramp. I think his children are parked out with a nurse. He

[1] My Colonel.

wouldn't do anything except stroll around and sleep or fish or anything of that kind.

The pantomime's all printed now.

Love,
WILLIAM

We spent the summer of 1941 in the West Country. Then word came that the regiment, hitherto an infantry unit, was to change to tanks. This necessitated all and sundry going off in various directions on courses. I found myself on an armoured fighting vehicle course at Bovington in Dorset.

A.F.V. School,
Bovington,
Dorset
Sunday, Aug. 17th, 1941

Dear Pa and Ma,

Thanks very much for letters. You can't expect any German, remotely fond of his country, to accept a peace of any sort when he knows his country's going to be disarmed, especially in view of what happened in the last war. A German who would accept it – and would lead his disarmed country into cooperation with us after the war – would have to be a super-Pétain, because we'll be asking him to do even more in that line than Pétain does.

And I thought we didn't approve of Pétain. However, our point of view is most elastic.

Johnston[1] says Bridget should write to him whether she's got anything to say or not, as it's only civil to keep up with the old faces!

Love,
WILLIAM

[1] Brian Johnston was at the A.F.V. Camp.

A.F.V. School,
Bovington
Sunday, Aug. 24th, 1941

Dear Pa and Ma,

Johnston left yesterday. He's gone on leave for the next week to see his 'grey-haired'.

I get a week's leave about Sept. 20th, so I'll be slipping up then. I think we'll be going up to Yorkshire somewhere (hush!) then, but how long for I don't know. The course is going quite well. I know more about wireless than I did before.

They tell me I'm due to be signals officer, and I have 9 scout cars and 19 motor cycles under my command. The scout cars go backwards as fast as forwards. 45 m.p.h. Which suits me.

Love,
WILLIAM

September 3rd, 1941

Dear Pa and Ma,

Thanks very much for letters. I wonder if George has got his leave yet. I went to see him on Sunday and we went bathing again. He had to be on duty at 6 in the evening so we dropped him on the way back here.[1]

I gave my test lecture on wireless today and got a 'v.g.' I spent most of the time telling off the sergeant instructor for making me nervous when I'm tuning in.

Love,
WILLIAM

The course at Bovington was followed by an all-round course at Otley in Yorkshire about which my memory serves me not at all – so the chances are it was unpleasant.

[1] That was the last time I saw my brother George.

Otley
Thursday, Oct. 2nd, 1941

My dear Pa and Ma,

I'm living like Caesar in my tent. Tents in October! It's all right now because I've got lots of palliasses and groundsheets and what-not, but the first night was terrible.

There was an unfortunate moment last week when a man called Geoffrey Walker in the Buffs left his car for the day on the edge of the wood here – and the brakes of one of those big tanks failed on a slope nearby and it ran backwards and there was nothing left of the car in two seconds. The driver never knew he had run over anything.

These tanks go to a petrol station 8 miles from here to fill up, and they use 32 gallons to get there and back.

I had to lecture to the troops on American politics this afternoon!

Love,
WILLIAM

At the conclusion of this course I rejoined the regiment in Eastbourne where it was now stationed, with its new tanks chewing up the pavements of the town.

141 Rgt. RAC,
Oakwood Court,
Bolsover Road,
Eastbourne
Nov. 11th, 1941

Dear Pa and Ma,

That is our CORRECT address for the future. We're working very hard trying to arrange courses for all these people. I suppose they'll settle down soon. Generals keep inspecting us and saying 'Welcome to the Tanks, boys'! I share an office with the Adjutant because he has a gigantic room but I think I'll be moving out soon. We don't get much work done. The Colonel's in quite good form. He's going to perform in a concert at Christmas.

I didn't listen to Churchill's speech last night but it read much as usual.

We were inspected by a general today and he stopped and had a chat with me about wireless. I giggled slightly during the march just because the Sergeant Major was out of step, but it wasn't noticed.

Love,
WILLIAM

Sunday, 21st Dec. 1941

Dear Pa and Ma,

I tried to ring you up last night but there was a long delay and so I cancelled it at ten.

We've just finished one officers' course. Our schemes were great sport. I had to summon the Adjutant by wireless from Brighton to Lewes because he asked permission to go to a *thé dansant* while his truck was passing through the town.

The wirelesses work very well except when the hills are too high. The Colonel has had one fitted in his car, so we'll have to moderate our language now.

Love,
WILLIAM

Eastbourne
Dec. 28th, 1941

Dear Pa and Ma,

I'm afraid I forgot one of your birthdays but I've remembered the Earl's on 29th. Many happy returns for both.

I'm Orderly Officer today and I've been asleep in the office all day. The Padre asked the Colonel if I could play bridge this afternoon in the Orderly Room and he said he wasn't going to have the place turned into a gaming saloon.

Hoping you're all very well.

Love,
WILLIAM

Eastbourne
25/1/42

Dear Dadda and Mamma,

Thanks very much for letters. I may call you up tonight as I'm Orderly Officer. I went to Brighton last night, and saw Vivien Leigh in *Doctor's Dilemma* by Mr Shaw. Very good indeed.

Major Coates is C.O. as the Colonel's away. He's wonderful. He played bridge the other night. He said 'Why must I go two no trumps to show my hand's not good? Why can't I say I've got a damned awful hand?'

If there are any spare pheasants Col. Reid M.C., Capt. Hayward and Lt. Tracey might be a good idea, but not unless there are any spare. The others were all well received.

Love,
WILLIAM

Eastbourne
7/2/42

Dear Pa and Ma,

Thanks very much for letters. I had a letter from Alec saying he thought it foolish to stand as an Independent. I can't agree. What with one thing and another, in the place I'm thinking of going to, there might be a good chance. I'll see to it that it costs me very little. That is, if it comes off at all. It may not. The Colonel wrote and applied for permission in the right quarter. He seemed unmoved about my being an Independent; in fact he entirely agrees that the method of selecting candidates nowadays is disquieting.

I'll let you know what happens.

Love,
WILLIAM

That letter marks the start of my political career in uniform. My attitude towards the war was hardening. Far from my sanguine prophecies of days gone by, I saw it going on for ever. Rudoph Hess's flight from Germany had made no difference. Mr Churchill had not seen fit to enlighten us as to why he had come. All went on as before. I longed to break the deadlock, not just between warring nations, but also in Parliament.

The party truce disquieted me acutely since it meant no opposition voice was likely to be raised against the war except by sitting members, of whom there were few of that persuasion; and prospective reinforcements for those few were certain not to be adopted by constituency party canvassers in favour of the party truce.

This meant that only as an Independent could a candidate horn in on an election. And it also meant he had to face the Coalition Government's united opposition – which reduced his chances of a win to practically nil. I therefore thought my brother Alec's view that it was foolish to stand as an Independent ill-considered from my point of view. I kept my eye on a constituency up in Glasgow. When the writ was issued I went before the Colonel, much to his amusement and disgust. The Adjutant informed him that he had to send my application in to the War Office, which he duly did – after pronouncing imprecautions in the cheerful military manner – against politicians of all parties.

The Buffs
Wednesday, Feb. 25th [1942]

Dear Pa and Ma,

Thanks very much for letters. Wireless sets have worked well so far – but we've got what's called a Battle Practice tomorrow and then they may not. I told the Colonel that you sent that salmon to appease him in case they didn't!

I've got permission from the Army Council to stand. It's a bit late but still it's worth trying, as Independents are rather popular nowadays.

I saw a golden plover on the lawn yesterday, ten yards from the front door, cars, etc.

Love,
WILLIAM

Then came the by-election up in Glasgow. Some dynamic individuals got in touch with me when I arrived and gave me their support. Thanks to them I got my nomination papers lodged in time. Twelve citizens had signed for me at the behest of a solicitor who gave his practice up for the duration so that he could be my agent.

Three days in the constituency were the most that I could manage in my military circumstances. Nonetheless, I finished second, on a platform of peace by negotiation and my new approach to foreign policy. Exhausted but elated, I returned to Eastbourne and reported to my parents from there.

The Buffs
Sunday, May 3rd, 1942

Dear Pa and Ma,

I gave the Colonel my press cuttings and he said he would have voted for me. They say from Glasgow, after seeing my poll, that without the danger of the split vote I would have got in. It was great sport, anyway.

I'm going on a Liaison Officer's course for a fortnight.

Love,
WILLIAM

There was another by-election looming up, this time in the south. With my throat still sore from speech-making in Glasgow, I was clearly seeking further punishment.

Tonbridge,
Kent
May 21st, 1942

Dear Pa and Ma,

Thanks very much for letters. We've been in a field for a week – night marches, etc. – and we start tomorrow.

About Windsor, I'm going to find out about it when this scheme is over. I've had one or two letters about it from guys in the constituency. It's a good spot for an Independent because there's been no election there for 13 years. I'm hoping to get financial support and won't do anything till I do. I'll call you up when I finish this scheme.

The Conservative Assoc. might of course consider adopting me if I go and see them.

We've been pretty wet through, but we're O.K. The Colonel's tank ran away yesterday. Had it not demolished a lorry, it would have shipped on through a conservatory in a maternity home, where several babies were taking the air.

Hoping you're all well.

Love,
WILLIAM

The Windsor Conservative Association, strange to say, did not adopt me. Indeed they adopted Charles Mott-Radclyffe who had been in the same house with me at Eton. He won by 2,000 odd votes, although I had saturated the citizens with speeches – six or seven a day. Not a bad result when one considers that the Coalition Government united in their opposition to me, sending letters to the voters of Windsor signed by all the leaders of the Coalition. Even Anthony Eden, from the Foreign Office, saw fit to send a personal letter on the eve of Polling Day to each constituent.

The count took place in Windsor Town Hall. Just before the declaration, the returning officer called Charlie and myself to his table. 'There are some spoilt papers here,' he said. 'Do either of you want to claim any of them?' We looked at the first one, across which was written in red ink 'Fuck the pair of you!' Faced with this show of spontaneous goodwill we laughed, shook hands and went our ways, he to the House of Commons, I back to my regiment in answer to a telegram signed by the Adjutant.

With scarcely any voice left, I returned to Ashford, Kent, exhausted but elated by the fact that I had notched up over 7,000 votes. My brother officers congratulated me on an honourable defeat. Then came the reckoning.

Oakwood Court,
Bolsover Road,
Eastbourne
May 24th [1942]

Dear Pa and Ma,

Here is the bill. I never thought the printing would come to that. Can't it be struck off my allowance for the future? It's a bit regrettable that it should be so big.

Had a nice 450-mile motor cycle trip the other day.

I won't stand again unless I can get hold of the cash.

Love,
WILLIAM

The bill was for the printing of my election address. Presumably my father was prepared to pay, although he disapproved of my activities.

However, his opposition to my policies was somewhat modified after he attended a dinner in Glasgow, at about the time when I was standing for Windsor, during which the Chief Constable leaned across the table and said, in a loud voice, 'Lord Home, was that one of your sons who stood here in the by-election in the spring?' 'It was,' my father said, extremely defensively. 'My men were solidly behind him,' said the policeman. At which everybody smiled, including my bewildered father.

Anyway, the bill was paid and life resumed its normal tenor. Then a telegram came from my parents to say that brother George was missing. Evidently he had gone out on a training flight in a formation of a few planes from Vancouver Island. None had returned; it was blamed on a deterioration in the weather. Still, I lived in hope.

Ashford,
Kent
– June 1942

Dear Dadda and Mamma,

Thanks for telegram. George may easily have come down in

the sea and been picked up by a ship. They all have rubber boats with them.

Anyway, you'll be hearing again soon from the man who cabled you. I have a feeling George is alright.

Love,
WILLIAM

But no one ever heard of George again – nor any of his colleagues. All were lost. My parents felt his loss acutely, as did we all. The youngest of the brood, and the most carefree, he had been a favourite in the family. Now he was gone, leaving only happy memories behind him and some exquisite bird photographs which he had taken up in Scotland on his leaves.

My next letter was from Worthing, to which town our tanks had travelled down the coast from Eastbourne. It contained a court martial story that I often heard my father tell afterwards. At least it helped to cheer him up a little.

141, R.A.C.,
Worthing

Dear Pa and Ma,

Thanks very much for letters. I'm taking next weekend off to go and be godfather to the ex-Adjutant's son at Sandhurst.

When I was doing my Orderly Officer I wrote a poem about the senior officers. Reid threatened to put me under arrest but they're all asking for copies.

What about that raid on Dieppe? Was it a good idea?

The most wonderful thing happened here the other day. A man who had stolen some razor blades was court martialled and one of our Majors was president of the court. The court sat at 10.30. The Major wanted to catch the 11.30 train to London to go on leave, so he hurried through the proceedings somewhat and sentenced the man to death by mistake.

The Brigadier was amazed to receive the documents.

Love,
WILLIAM

Forty or more years since that letter was written I hasten to add a postscript to the effect that the Brigadier took immediate steps to override the Major's verdict and substitute a fine of a few pence!

By-elections were still on my mind, and the policy of unconditional surrender was beginning to colour all my thinking. I believed then, and I still believe that to ask regular soldiers, fighting for their country (never mind who leads them), to surrender unconditionally is not the way to shorten any war.

As the German colonel in charge of all the Channel Islands said in a play of mine called *The Dame of Sark*, which I wrote many years later.

'What would your Mr Churchill say were somebody to ask him to surrender unconditionally?'

To which the Dame replied, 'I wouldn't like to think.'

141 R.A.C.
Ashford,
Kent
Aug. 15th [1942]

Dear Pa and Ma,

I think I'll be coming on leave around 25th August or 1st Sept. I'd rather like a nice by-election in the North at that time.

What are Churchill and Roosevelt up to now? I expect the Italians will close down soon. They certainly would if only we'd give them decent peace terms, instead of that ridiculous unconditional surrender racket.

I'll let you know exactly when I get leave.

Love,
WILLIAM

But no MP resigned his seat or kicked the bucket or was elevated to the peerage during the few weeks before I went on leave. And so I rested instead of electioneering during that leave and felt much the better for it, which accounts for the theatrical activity that winter in the regiment.

141 R.A.C.,
Worthing
Sept. 14th, 1942

Dear Pa and Ma,

I had a delightful leave and feel very well after it.

I had to see Reid today and he pointed out that I was rising up in seniority in the rgt. and I must stop pulling the senior officers' legs. He's not a bad old thing. He's not keen about an instructor's job, and believes in one staying where one is. He may be right.

Love,
WILLIAM

141 R.A.C.,
Worthing
25th September, 1942

Dear Pa and Ma,

Thanks for letters and grouse. They went down very well indeed. We're doing *Cinderella* for Christmas. I'm adapting it for a military background with Maj. Edmeades who's going to be General Prince Charming. I'm Cinderella and Reid's the Fairy Queen.

Are there any old military great-coats at Hirsel, because mine's getting a bit done?

Love,
WILLIAM

Ashford,
Kent
Oct. 6th, 1942

Dear Pa and Ma,

My wireless school is right out in the woods, and I take my

gun on my journeys to and fro by scout car. I've seen no good pigeon wood yet – though there are some birds about.

There's nowhere to go in the evening which appals some of the officers. A man caught a 23 lb. pike in the lake the other day. Have you any spare tackle?

Reid wants to be one of the Ugly Sisters instead of the Fairy Queen.

Love,
WILLIAM

By the end of the year I had been promoted captain. If the Germans were quailing at my military preparation, they didn't show it. Besides, by the following spring I was beset by more serious doubts.

141 R.A.C.
Ashford,
Kent
March 28th, 1943

My dear Pa,

I am seriously thinking of taking part in another by-election shortly as a 'Peace by Agreement' candidate. I have come to the conclusion that the war has outrun its usefulness, if it ever had any, and that the complete disarmament and surrender of the Nazi nations, and their consequent humiliation and setback to national pride, will ensure another war in 20 years. What is more, I think the only solution is a touch of internationalisation of strategic points etc., started by me. That being so, I find it very unsatisfactory being in the Army and having those views in private. In fact, people go so far as to say it's fundamentally dishonest.

I have no wish to leave the Army and what is more I see no reason why I should; but to set the conscience at rest, I'd like to lay my view before the public – in fact, I shan't be happy till I have.

Could you drop a line to Reid and tell him you understand I

intend to do this, as I'm not sure I dare tell him? The chances are he wouldn't mind, so long as I continue to render unto Caesar when not performing on the platform. My mind, such as it is, is made up on this point.

WILLIAM

The worry I had always had about my private view of war being in opposition to the view expected of me as a soldier was still there. My rise in rank, consistent with my wish to do my best once I had been conscripted, seemed to be creating a dual personality. Thus the peacemonger in me sought to balance things up. But it progressively became more difficult.

Bovington
May 9th, 1943

Dear Pa and Ma,

Thanks for letters. I go back on Wednesday. We're going training for a week, but letters to Ashford will find me.

My Squadron Commander who's very keen on cleanliness etc., looked in the mortar on one of my tanks and found a robin's nest with four eggs. As it was just before the Divisional General's inspection, he had the mortar removed from the tank and placed near it. I've not heard if the robin came back. However, it probably did, as during the laying period the tank went out on a two-day scheme and the robin returned, when the tank came back, and laid another egg. Many happy returns to Bridge for May 4.

Love,
WILLIAM

141 R.A.C.,
Ashford,
Kent
June 4th, 1943

Dear Pa and Ma and Bridget,

My report from the Battle School said I was 'brilliant but

sarcastic and lighthearted' and the Div. Commander wrote: 'Any officer however brilliant who does not pull his weight on course is no good to me. Any further complaints about this officer, he will be removed.' Pompous old nitwit.

I had my inoculation last night and am spending the day till dinner time in bed. The doctor told me I am short-sighted, so I'll be wearing hornrims when you see me next.

Love,

WILLIAM

To judge from future events, the Divisional Commander was not such a 'pompous old nitwit' as I thought at the time!

Life went on much the same as usual, with my new job keeping me employed full time and stopping me from brooding too much on the conduct of the war.

Colonel Reid departed, to be replaced by a Scottish international rugger player called Waddell. He gave my suede shoes a fairly searching glance, then – improbably – made me Adjutant. We toiled through a succession of schemes and exercises (on one of which I read 1,051 pages of *War and Peace*), we saw photographs of Churchill wearing a fur hat to cheer up the Russians, we even had an Irish Sergeant Major who was betting the war would be over by Christmas.

141 R.A.C.,
Ashford,
Kent
Sept. 8th, 1943

Dear Pa and Ma,

I got a sleeper! Had a delightful leave.

I got back to find a letter awaiting me from Waddell, who is on leave, to say that he requires a new Adjutant who has been a businessman. Having expressly stated when he asked me to be Adjutant that he didn't want a clerk, and having since discovered that no man needs a clerk more, I'm not really surprised.

Still, it's a bit annoying to ask somebody to do something

and then remove them by post. It's also annoying as it gave me something to do, and I've nothing to do in the squadron. However I'll see how things do go for a bit, and bear in mind that the Phantom Reconnaissance Regiment, in which all my buddies are, is a good spot.

He had the grace to say no one had ever worked so hard. He was right there. But he tried to do everybody's job which infuriated me, and I pointed it out somewhat tactfully to him in my answer.

Hoping you're all very well.

Love,
WILLIAM

Back in a squadron, with comparative leisure leaving me a lot of time in which to brood on politics again, my urge to fight a by-election once again took over.

141 R.A.C.,
Ashford,
Kent
Sept. 24th, 1943

My dear Pa and Ma,

I have decided to stand as an Independent at St Albans – and applied for permission. Can I produce £150 for my nomination? It's on the question of unconditional surrender and I cannot rest until I've found out if it's as unpopular with the public as it is with me. It seems completely unnecessary to carry on the war until we've had a good Old Testament peace – which never led anywhere – and I'm quite sure many people agree with me. St Albans looks as good as anywhere, though I shall certainly be beaten. Still, that doesn't matter if one gets the thing over.

Love,
WILLIAM

Though I had applied for permission to stand for St Albans, it failed to come through until too late.

Ashford,
Kent
Oct. 9th [1943]

Dear Pa and Ma,

Sorry I haven't written for so long, but as you know I've been out on a scheme. We've just got back. It's quite interesting about my permission for St Albans. Lots of people seem to think that they sat on it on purpose, and I expect we'll hear more about it. Pardon the publicity!

There were staff officers chasing all round the downs in every direction on nomination day, but I had been taken prisoner – by the BLUE nations, and it was too late when they got me.

I've quite a lot of letters from St Albans and wouldn't have done too badly. However a nice Glasgow seat in the near future should not do me any harm – if there's one going.

Love,
WILLIAM

It was during this period that an accident occurred on one of our schemes in which live ammunition was used on the downs which very nearly put paid to my account. I was ordered to go as a liaison officer with the infantry, on foot, rather than in my tank, as was the normal custom.

Off I went with a sergeant and, as we approached a wood high on the downs, shells from the supporting artillery started exploding all around us and in the wood ahead, killing a few infantry soldiers who had already reached it. We hurriedly took cover in some bushes and wirelessed back to stop the barrage. After what seemed hours, but was probably only a few minutes, the gunfire stopped.

Ashford,
Kent
Feb. [?], 1944

Dear Pa and Ma,

I'm going to become a Liberal. They are delighted to have me, and I'm going to call on them one day.

I see Mr Churchill has been writing rude letters to the electors of Brighton. When will he learn?

I'm still working out the court martial of an Artillery captain I'm defending. We've got 19 witnesses for the defence including Canadian officers, bus conductors and an American officer!

Could Collingwood[1] get me some shirts and pyjamas. I could send the coupons.

Love,
WILLIAM

141, R.A.C.,
Ashford,
Kent
20th March, 1944

Dear Pa and Ma,

Thanks very much for letters. I am going to Clay Cross tomorrow to have a look round. I feel bound to try there. I'll endeavour to keep the financial situation well under control.

However, Mr Churchill has gone too far saying the Atlantic Charter does not apply to Germany, and I can't remain silent.

I'll be getting leave soon and I'll call up to see you.

Love,
WILLIAM

Clay Cross was (and still is) a strong Labour seat, but I thought it would probably be my last chance to stand as a Parliamentary candidate in this world. I knew the Second Front was just about to start and I was convinced that I would not get leave to fight a by-election – should there be one – from the battlefield.

I went to Clay Cross with a corporal from my regiment to help me. He gave up his leave to do so but his sacrifice, though noble, did not help me to save my deposit.

[1] My parents' butler.

This depressed me greatly – not so much the losing of the deposit, but the fact that the Labour voters in Clay Cross voted for a Labour candidate who preached an alien creed – namely the war aims of the Coalition Government, its policy of unconditional surrender, its insistence that the Atlantic Charter should not apply to Germany. I thought my view might be more in sympathy. But I lost not only my deposit but my voice as well.

The build-up to the Second Front was now progressing fast.

'R' Sqdn.,
141, R.A.C.,
A.P.O., England
April 23rd, 1944

Dear Pa and Ma,

Thanks very much for letters. You will observe that my address is changed and will only necessitate a 1½d stamp! Part of the war of nerves. It's lovely weather here. The magnolias are looking very nice.

There was a good deal of ribaldry when I got back after the election. I was absolutely exhausted, but Waddell refused to give me leave. Instead he's made me a squadron commander of all the crooks in the regt. Half of them haven't arrived yet because they're all in detention!

Ask Ma to write to Mrs Tucker, 47 High St., Clay Cross for feeding me like a mother.

Love,
WILLIAM

'R' Sqdn.,
141, R.A.C.,
A.P.O., England
May 6th, 1944

Dear Pa and Ma,

I am living in a tent, surrounded by this crowd of roughs. I administer justice every morning to the punishment of wickedness and vice from an upper room in a cottage with no windows and a hole in the roof.

Waddell is away, but keeps ringing me up. I can't understand what he says, but I answer at random.

This Army Post Office takes about ten days to deliver letters. They don't seem to have very much method or interest in whether they deliver letters correctly or not. Thanks very much for guarantee.[1] I think it's all paid now.

Love to Bridgetina.

WILLIAM

269 Fwd. Dely. Sqdn.
A.P.O., England
May 21st, 1944

Dear Pa and Ma,

That's my new address. I hope you are all keeping well. Reid is around here. I shall visit him one day. He didn't go to Edinburgh as Welfare Officer after all. When's the Second Front?

It's raining and very cold today. Ryle[2] tells me he's getting married. As he's got most of my shirts and all my socks and undies, he should be well fitted out for a trousseau.

The hour is approaching when I must go out for a glass of wine.

Love,
WILLIAM

269 Fwd. Dely. Sqdn.,
A.P.O., England
June 6th, 1944

Dear Pa and Ma,

Thanks very much for telegram and letters. And please thank Bridget for her letter. I hear on the wireless that the Second Front has begun! I suppose the day will come when I

[1] Of the overdraft incurred by my expenses at Clay Cross.

[2] A fellow officer.

shall attend it. By the way, the *Forward* Delivery Squadron is not the Food Delivery Sqdn. – Mamma. My Sqdn. Cmdr. is deeply hurt that he should be taken for a member of the Army Catering Corps, though the mistake is quite understandable.

I went to Windsor Races on Saturday.

I've got most of my clothes back from Ryle now.

I had dinner with Mary Churchill last night and pointed out the errors of her father's ways. She said that if I argued with him, he would say, 'Young man, you darken counsel' – whatever that may mean.

Love,
WILLIAM

269 Fwd. Dely. Sqdn.,
A.P.O., England
June 11th, 1944

Dear Pa and Ma,

Thanks very much for telegram on my birthday. How do you think the invasion is going? I hear that some comedians concealed themselves in slit trenches, fondly imagining they were invisible, quite close to the Germans, and an old lady insisted on giving them breakfast on a tray!

I'll write again soon. I expect letters are a bit delayed nowadays. They'll probably get delayed still more soon.

Love,
WILLIAM

269 Fwd. Dely. Sqdn.,
A.P.O., England
June 17th, 1944

Dear Pa and Ma,

Thanks very much for letters which arrive at irregular intervals. Waddell has eaten about 2 tons of strawberries in the last few days. He'll be getting a rash soon.

I see the King and W. Churchill have visited the beaches –

to say nothing of General de Gaulle. They say it's like Cowes Regatta over there.

I'd like to see that pied flycatcher. I expect it's in the same place as before. When are these peace terms coming along?

Love,
WILLIAM

That letter was the last I wrote from England to my parents. The next came from Northern France, arriving on 4 July after a long delay.

269 Fwd. Dely. Sqdn.,
c/o A.P.O., B.W.F.

My dear Pa and Ma,

Thanks very much for the copies of Shakespeare. They are just the right size and I will be able to carry them around with me. I haven't seen General de Gaulle yet but the French people seem to be very very far from starving. Presumably either the Gestapo or our propaganda has slipped up.

The crossing was uneventful – the weather was wonderful. Lots of swifts about, but there's not much flying space for them in view of the colossal number of aeroplanes around. I suppose I'm enjoying myself in a way, but in a very strange way. Thank Bridget very much for her letter. You might write and let me know when the war's over. I doubt if anyone will tell us here.

Love,
WILLIAM

269 Fwd. Dely. Sqdn.
June 21st, 1944

Dear Pa and Ma,

I haven't had any letters for a week, but did not expect them. How are you all keeping? It looks as though Cherbourg will be taken very soon now.

The nearer one gets to the war, the more I wish I was having a nice quiet leave at Hirsel. Jakie Astor sent me a cheque for £150 the other day towards the election expenses. Very nice of him, and has eased the situation quite a bit.

I wonder how long the war is going on for? Henry should have the latest information.

I'll write again as soon as possible and let you know how things are going.

Love,
WILLIAM

The cheque from Jakie Astor (now Sir J.J.) was delivered to me on my landing craft as it left Gosport, the post corporal throwing it over the side of the boat as we sailed. There was a covering letter which contained the phrase 'You talk a lot of balls but at least you talk!' The following letters all speak for themselves.

269 Fwd. Dely. Sqdn.,
B.W.E.F.
June 28th [1944]

Dear Pa and Ma,

I'm still O.K. A little white wine last night from a farmer and some eggs. He said the Germans took everything but he had more chickens and ducks than I've seen in years. I have been sitting around in a field sleeping most of the time since I've been here – getting more and more depressed.

Plenty of redstarts about, otherwise rooks and an occasional warbler. I wish I was watching the flycatcher with you by Dunglass Bridge. Tell Alec that our peace terms in detail, omitting unconditional surrender, would be welcomed by all troops on both sides out here. The Germans are merely fighting for the honour of their army now. That's nothing new. On the other hand unconditional surrender is a figment of Mr Churchill's over-heated brain. Most of the prisoners are 17 or 18 years old. The officers very smart with batmen – not that I've seen any of them yet – or indeed anything.

Love,
WILLIAM

269 Fwd. Dely. Sqdn.,
B.W.E.F.

Dear Pa and Ma,

I had a letter from Bridget today. Don't be worried if you don't get any letters from me for some time because postage will be difficult and opportunities for writing few. There are moments when I loathe this war almost to the point of despair and times when I can adjust myself to it. The latter are becoming more frequent. However, it all makes one realise what a wonderful life you have provided for your vast family after the war. I trust I shall be less selfish and intolerant. The solution really is not to think at all, except about the moment. I saw a redstart yesterday in an orchard here and a duck. It's rumoured that Col. Reid may be here soon in August. I missed Henry's[1] broadcast. The country around here is very beautiful – and like Kent. A Frenchman came and asked me if I had stolen a cow yesterday! The answer was no.

The weather is very good apart from thunder-showers which drench one to the skin in a few minutes. I'm glad my clothes have arrived all right. I expect Collingwood is fussing about them.

Love,
WILLIAM

The Buffs. (R.A.C.),
B.W.E.F.
July 4th, 1944

Dear Pa and Ma,

I have been getting quite a few letters, but, as they are all addressed A.P.O. England, it looks as though you have not had any from me on this side. It keeps raining all the time, otherwise I personally have nothing to report. In the orchard in which I live in one corner, there are blackcaps, bullfinches,

[1] Brother Henry broadcast on birds from Edinburgh.

redstarts, chaffinches, magpies, warblers. There are quite a lot of French people around here and I'm told they are coming back daily through the German lines to what is left of their homes, which in some places is nothing. I cannot see this battle going right through France devastating everything in the name of liberation. Somebody will complain, and I notice Gen. de Gaulle does not exactly associate himself with the effort for fear of post-war repercussions. I hope Alec was not attacked by a doodle-bug while he was in London. I have come to the conclusion that I do not like war. My nerves are perpetually on edge. I assume that every gun which goes off and every aeroplane which flies is assigned exclusively to me.

You will notice my new address. We have dropped the 141 part. As George VI remarked to our Brigadier once, 'There is no *esprit de corps* in a number.' I thought of asking him why he was called George VI. I have just drunk a huge whisky and soda at 1100 hours in the morning as a farewell to the Major commanding the camp. I am leaving for another one further *back*.

Love,
WILLIAM

The Buffs. R.A.C.,
B.W.E.F.
July 5th, 1944

Dear Pa and Ma,

Discussing the war with an ex-actor officer[1] in this regiment we have come to the conclusion that it is a rather sordid revival of the last one. Like a very out of date musical comedy being played before an apathetic audience. The weather is magnificent now. We have a tame young magpie in the Mess which gazes into space like a bishop trying to remember the text of his sermon.

There is a colossal amount of dairy produce in this area, which we are allowed to buy. Meat, bread, etc., however, are

[1] Raymond Westwell.

not allowed, as the French are short and the Germans keep sending back the refugees through their lines.

I see Sir Samuel Hoare has retired from Chelsea. I doubt if that by-election will take place before the end of the war, which I hope will be very soon.

I understand that one of the mail boats with early letters ran into another ship. It may or may not be true. There are more rumours than Germans around here.

Love,
WILLIAM

141 R.A.C. The Buffs,
B.W.E.F.
July 12th, 1944

Dear Pa and Ma,

Thanks very much for letters. They are coming through all right now. The weather is bad again. I have been leading a very quiet life. One of our young officers who loves playing around with explosives found a square of earth which had been dug up yesterday. He said it was an anti-tank mine, and put some explosive in the hole to blow it up, and a huge shower of rather inferior Bromo appeared from a privy which the previous people in the camp had built according to the rule of Hygiene!

I have got almost impervious to bad news now, when one hears about one's friends. I am still capable, however, of considering that this war has gone on far too long, and political propaganda, such as the Americans used at Cherbourg could save millions of lives. As I keep repeating, the Germans are fighting for their honour and because they don't know what to expect. It is criminal not to (a) give them our terms, and (b) make sure that they know they will be treated justly. They just do NOT know now.

I haven't seen the Colonel for a few days. He looks at me with open-eyed wonder nowadays, because he finds me so remarkably unwarlike.

The pilot of an aeroplane parachuted out of his aeroplane over the Mess the other day. The Mess Sgt. prepared a gin and lemon for him, but the wind wafted him away too far.

Love,

WILLIAM

141 R.A.C. (The Buffs),
B.L.A.
(British Liberating Army!)
July 17th, 1944

Dear Pa and Ma,

Many thanks for letters. I saw a woodpecker yesterday with black and white bars on its back. Either it was a lesser spotted woodpecker or it had had itself painted with stripes like the Allied aircraft.

It's very, very hot today. The Brigadier thought my thesis on Propaganda had a lot in it. I await its final destination. Everybody's walking about with bathing drawers only. I presume Churchill is seeing Roosevelt now. May they reach some constructive conclusion. Otherwise Europe will disintegrate for 200 years. Proof that the Germans are only fighting for their honour accumulates daily. One (a colonel) refused to surrender until someone produced a tank, so they drove one up to his H.Q. and he said 'Now I have been subjected to a tank attack. Honour is satisfied.' Childish, but pride is childish, and that is all that keeps them going. It would be easy to neutralise it if it wasn't for the fact that our statesmen suffer from the same complaint.

ENSA is here now, giving Stars in Battledress performance. Let me know when there's a by-election in Scotland and I'll come back and fight it. If Marshal von Kluge is wanted by the Russians as a war criminal, I should have thought he would have preferred to hand himself over to us. Evidently not, though doubtless it is in the back of his mind.

Love,

WILLIAM

B.L.A.
July 23rd, 1944

Dear Pa and Ma,

Thank you very much for letters. Weather has been foul here lately. As I live in a deep hole, for no particular reason, I find myself floating about in water. Churchill was seen in the area a few days ago. He never called on me, but I presume he knows my views on his politics without interview.

The letter Mr Stokes[1] quoted in the House the other day was from me, unless somebody else used identical words and phrases, which seems unlikely. Unfortunately, he described the writer as having fought all the way from El Alamein! He must have meant Cathcart.

I am very interested in the news, or lack of it, from Germany. If only they would give an ounce of encouragement to the German generals, instead of calling them rude names, they could close the war down in a week. They dropped a lot of leaflets the other night quoting from ill-considered speeches in the past by Churchill and Smuts.

Our doctor saw a barrage balloon lying in a field the other day. Wanting something to keep his blankets in, he slipped out of his car and was about to cut it up when he realised it was about to be blown up for use.

I see that Marshal von Kluge has said he will hold firm in the West. They say he's rather a fine man, although he's wanted by the Russians as a war criminal, but then who isn't? Where are those peace terms?

Love,
WILLIAM

B.L.A.
July 28th, [1944]

Dear Pa and Ma,

Thank you very much for letters. Things go on here very much as usual.

[1] Dick Stokes, Labour MP.

I have not yet had my interview with the head of the Psychological Warfare Department. He seems difficult to find. In any case, I expect he's hamstrung by the obstinacy of W. Churchill.

There is a lot of criticism out here of this failure to produce terms when the Second Front opened, to say nothing of the failure to support the anti-Hitler boys the other day. When the war is won it will be in spite of the politicians, not because of them. They are doing everything they can to stiffen German resistance and consequently causing unnecessary casualties.

I wish Alec would do something about it by writing to some sympathetic newspaper. It really is acute, and every day a few hundred more soldiers and civilians are killed – for what?

I have an acting Sgt. Major in my Sqdn. who checks 20 men every morning 'for having long hair', cuts it himself in the evening, and makes 5 francs out of each!

Love,
WILLIAM

B.L.A.
July 31st, 1944

Dear Pa and Ma,

Thanks very much for letters. I had one from Bridget yesterday as well. The weather is magnificent. They have now fixed an interview for me with the Director of Psychological Warfare. It took them a fortnight to find him.

There's a man attached to us who used to work with Welch's garage in Coldstream. I had a chat with him today. We've also got a sergeant who was a bookie in peace time. He said George Lambton[1] was the straightest trainer there had ever been. And the most frequently bankrupt!

Ryle is a major now – and still wearing my panties! He says you are not to worry, quoting the old saying 'He that hath two pairs of pants let him give to him that hath none'. To

[1] Mother's uncle.

which I reply 'And from him that hath none, shall be taken away even that which he hath.' Thus getting nowhere, and he still continues to wear my panties.

Somebody drove my jeep up a telegraph pole the other day, but it is being repaired and should return today. I haven't seen a German yet. However, I'm visiting one of our officers in hospital today, and in his tent there is a German officer who sits polishing his Iron Cross all day with a broad grin. I understand he is pleased to be sitting there instead of being shot, as he suspected he would be.

Rachel has rather knocked off correspondence since I wrote her a fruity one about politics. I find the new padre agrees with me that 'unconditional surrender' is costing thousands of unnecessarily expended lives.

Some of our people have gone home because their homes have been blasted by 'doodle-bugs'. You might get Collingwood to put a couple of cartridges in the boiler.

I don't want any cigarettes, thank you, Ma. We get plenty of tobacco around here, and, as I've previous remarked, the country is rich with provender. I believe they are going to ration the inhabitants to feed the Parisians, who've doubtless also got a lot of food hidden away under their beds.

It's said that Rommel has been wounded. That may or may not be so. The Americans are advancing fast. They took a whole battalion intact the other day, by sending back a prisoner with a few well-chosen words and suggestions. They seem to choose their words a little better than we do.

The doctor has now built himself a tent out of two ends of a marquee, which he stole out of an ordnance camp. He comes from Ireland. It looks like an aeroplane without wings. He told the Colonel that sailing was the best exercise for the men to do in the afternoons. As the sea is some distance away the suggestion was not well received.

Hoping you are all very well. I'll write again in a day or two.

Love,
WILLIAM

B.L.A.
Aug. 3rd, 1944

Dear Pa and Ma,

I got letters from you both this morning. Thanks very much. It *was* me that Stokes quoted in the H of C the other day. I got a letter from him this morning!

The weather is very good again. I still haven't had my interview with the Psychological Warfare gents yet, but I had to give them all my particulars yesterday. The war will probably be over before they do anything about it.

I had to play basket-ball with Wadd last night. He's usually out for weeks on end, but he's been hanging round here lately – most exhausting. He asked me to scrub his back in the shower bath and then asked if I thought it degrading. I replied, 'It's a great honour, sir.'

He has more or less written me off as a fighting soldier. It's his own fault. In spite of telling him my views, he used to say 'Home, you talk like this in England, but when you get over there you'll be keen to fight – you'll be a wild man!' He found out his mistake. If I don't get the Psych. job I've offered to drive his Staff Car for him. He said, 'That'd be more embarrassing for me than it would for you', adding, 'I've been very decent to you, Home. I could have had you court martialled twice in the last six months, but I didn't – and you jib at scrubbing my back!'

They say the war goes well at the front. People are a bit too optimistic. Mr Eden's emphasis yesterday on 'unconditional surrender' made me feel faintly sick. Even the Bavarian officer in the hospital still has his pride, and it must be taken into account.

I listened to W.C.'s speech – medieval stuff with one or two thinly disguised falsehoods about equipment.

I have now persuaded our Communist corporal that Stalin and Hitler and Churchill will all come to grief because they allow no opposition. He's convinced about the last two only.

Love,
WILLIAM

141 R.A.C.,
The Buffs,
B.L.A.
Aug. 8th, 1944

Dear Pa and Ma,

Thanks very much for letters. Please thank Bridget.

I got a copy of *Hansard* from Stokes. It's nice to be quoted with Churchill and Smuts. Not their current opinions, of course.

They say in the papers the war is going well. It's confirmed by the ENSA parties when they come back from the front. I'm still sitting in the same orchard, less one tree I demolished with the doctor yesterday. We've discovered an enormous dead poplar we intend to strike down, but it's on the edge of a rather angry Frenchman's garden.

I saw the Psych. Warfare man. Unfortunately he comes from the Foreign Office, so he's no use to me.

A German colonel said if the invasion had been two months later it would have failed, because Rommel was getting a move on. Before he came they had been lying about sun-bathing and doing no defences (including the colonel).

It's a lovely day today and has been for some time. Dew in the morning, but in my hole I don't notice it. Incidentally, I'm the only person in this area who dreams of sleeping underground, and my subterranean house is viewed by visitors as thought it were the Leaning Tower of Pisa.

I'm glad to see von Rundstedt hasn't been shot. They say he's a good chap. On the other hand, he may be just as obstinate as Mr C.

Look out for a by-election for me.

Love,
WILLIAM

By now a by-election was imminent in the Borderland. I wrote to Uncle Claud (Lambton), my mother's brother, asking for his support.

B.L.A.
Aug. 12th, 1944

My dear Claud,

You will get in touch with the Liberal Association forthwith and persuade them that I, W. Home, having fought for liberation for the last three years against stupendous odds, am the man who is required as their candidate. Having used your telephone properly, you will sit down and answer *by return*, what you have achieved.

Go to it!

Love,
WILLIAM

B.L.A.
Aug. 13th, 1944

My dear Pa and Ma,

Thanks very much for letters. Weather still marvellous. Everybody very optimistic except me, knowing as I do, with that uncanny political perception that I have, that the war will only begin the day it ends.

I hope you will see to it that I get that seat. Was not grandpapa M.P. for that area? What more fitting? I expect a great deal of work to be done on my behalf in the next few days. I have issued operational orders to Henry and Bridget and Claud. Claud may be a quisling – and one or two others.

I read Montgomery's message to troops in the *Daily Express*.

I also read an order issued by a German divisional commander saying that pilfering and so-called 'purchase with a show of weapons' would be very seriously punished.

I did *not* read that in the *Daily Express*.

Two very old French ladies from the chateau nearby came in a donkey cart to listen to the news last night. I fed the donkey on sour apples when they weren't looking and heard a dull explosion later in the night.

One of our officers was going to England by plane last night, but he gave up his seat to two American airmen who had walked all the way from Germany.

Waddell is turning a 3-ton lorry into a caravan. He went to hospital the other day because he was suffering from Tiglath.[1] The doctor told him he wasn't fit, and escaped with his life only because he was at Glasgow University when young.

Love,

WILLIAM

B.L.A.

Aug. 17th, 1944

Dear Pa and Ma,

I am living on the edge of a stream and there are two kingfishers which hang around about ten yards away.

Went to see a brigadier running Propaganda at Army H.Q. yesterday. He said they have no jobs at present but would bear my name in mind. They grind slowly, these people.

We found a foal of a racehorse which had fallen into a bomb hole and strained its back. We are feeding it on grass and biscuits. It must have been cut by shrapnel a few weeks ago as it has several wounds. The doctor visits it thrice daily and rubs creosote into it. It's doing well and may win the Derby one day. We are going to keep it if possible.

What about Berwick? Have you fixed that yet?

Hoping you are all very well.

Love,

WILLIAM

B.L.A.

Aug. 21st, [1944]

Dear Pa and Ma,

Thanks very much for letters.

Everyone has got a private car or so, and most of the British Army consists of German vehicles left behind. I've just asked

[1] Pseudonym for piles.

an officer to go and get me a nice car – but he hasn't come back yet. I expect him to have a Ford V8. I'm glad to report that our horse is all right now and walked away without a word of thanks. They say the war is going well, but the Germans show no sign of giving in. They have no reason to – I've always said so. So long as you have a pseudo-Field-Marshal conducting your political affairs you will find the war going on until the last shot. That goes for both sides.

Hoping you're very well.

Love,
WILLIAM

Uncle Claud wrote a rude letter to me in response to my request that he should intervene on my behalf in Berwick. I replied:

141, R.A.C.,
The Buffs,
B.L.A.
August 21st, 1944

You foul and constipated sea-lion,

How dare you speak like that to me.

What of your hero, W. Churchill, who has joined more political parties than he's had glasses of brandy? What of him?

And do not say I have embraced every political creed when you know full well that I have been an Independent no less than three times with EXACTLY the same election address each time and exactly the same motto – which is 'Stop this war' – and only different slogans to stir the imagination of the massed constipation which one sees around one.

And pause to consider what you mean when you say *I* have cooked *my* political goose as an Atlantic Charter candidate. Is it not a sad commentary on the distortion of the human mind that I – the only man in three continents to stick up for a solemn declaration made by three so-called statesmen, and since overthrown by them – should be told I have finished my political career?

Must one then, for a political career, be doomed to hang onto the coat tails of these unspeakable old criminals as they change their minds and promise this and tear up that and slaughter half a continent the while?

Ah, Lambton, Lambton. Is re-education only to take place in Germany?

A joke now am I? 'You laught at me now, but the day will come when you will hear my words.' That man, Disraeli, saved his country from at least three wars.

Ponder these things, young man.

I have not seen a German yet. I'm told the war is going well.

Give my love to the wife and daughter.

And as for Hitler – he was a dictator more interested in military than political affairs. He would not be contradicted. He refused to discuss anything with his enemies. To teach them a lesson he relied exclusively on force.

The chief difference is that he did not smoke cigars or wear a sailor suit.

Love,
WILLIAM

141, R.A.C.,
(The Buffs),
B.L.A.
Sept. 1st, 1944

Dear Pa and Ma,

Thanks very much for letters. I haven't written much lately because we've been on the move so fast. We had a wireless link stretching for 75 miles in our one regiment, so you can imagine how they move. I have been sitting in for the Adjutant this afternoon while he's out stealing fruit.

There's a burnt out tank or lorry every twenty yards on every road. Most astonishing, and nothing smells quite so revolting as a dead horse. Major Edmeades drives in his jeep with his handkerchief out, exactly like Lady Home visiting one of her children with 'flu! It's time we had a little dose of peace terms now – I had a letter from Alec yesterday or the day before.

I expect Col. Reid'll be out here soon, except that he always makes public the fact that he loathes all foreigners.

Hoping you're all very well. I can't get an afternoon's sleep in nowadays because small French children about two feet high keep coming into my tent and shaking me warmly by the hand.

A cow went into Waddell's tent last night and ate his sponge.

Love,
WILLIAM

141 R.A.C.,
(The Buffs),
B.L.A.
Sept. 8th, 1944

Dear Pa and Ma,

I am afraid I have got myself into trouble. I have refused an order to go and attack Le Havre. I spent the whole of last night thinking about it, and decided to do so.

I do hope you won't be upset. Probably there will be no trouble about it – on the other hand I might be court martialled and dismissed from the Service.

You have always been very tolerant about my point of view and, after all, it's the only consistent end to my useless army career. It's entirely their own fault for keeping me in it. I've made repeated requests to Waddell to let me go and he wouldn't. I applied to resign my commission when I saw how the 'unconditional surrender' racket was causing unnecessary casualties, and he held up the application.

However he's very friendly – as is everybody.

It's quite unnecessary to attack the foul place. It's purely to allow some politician to say all France is liberated. As a port it will be useless for some time. The German Commander offered to send out all civilians, if he was given three days. It was refused. That was four days ago and the battle hasn't started yet. The thousands of casualties there'll be could have been utilised to keep the Germans in there till the end of the war – not that they have the least desire to get out.

Don't worry about this letter. I've been blowing up for it for years and it's a certain relief to let out the gas.

You will probably think that I have made a great mistake. On the other hand you may think it was inevitable.

It may well be that nothing will come of it at all.

I saw no less than 25 white German ambulances on one road – and they *were* ambulances – which had been blown up by Typhoons, and then the Rev. W. H. Elliot had the effrontery to say that the Germans have overthrown the Red Cross.

C'est la guerre – mais ce n'est pas magnifique!

Love,
WILLIAM

I refer to my repeated requests to the Colonel to be allowed to resign my commission. I had not mentioned them in earlier letters because I had not wanted to worry my parents. Looking back on it, the shock they got from reading that last letter might have been less violent had I done so.

Nonetheless they took it well, God bless them.

B.L.A.
Sept. 10th, 1944

Dear Pa and Ma,

Thanks for letters received tonight. I bought this fountain pen for 200 francs. There have been no further developments over the disturbance, except that the Colonel has ordered me to stay in an orchard here for a few days. I don't really regret my action. After all, from the start I've had a point of view which would either prove itself irresistible at the '*moment critique*' or not. Well, it has.

I doubt if I will be court martialled because the Colonel

held up an application to resign my commission, which he shouldn't have done, and nobody wants to get him into trouble, least of all myself. I seem fated to get into trouble – doubtless entirely my own fault.

I went off in a German car with the doctor the other day, with no brakes, and no engine cover. Due to mechanical difficulties we spent the night in a French farmhouse, and drank a bottle of brandy.

Well, I hope you are all well. I wrote a letter to the *Maidenhead Advertiser* last week, which they published in two columns.

Love,
WILLIAM

B.L.A.
Sept. 17th, 1944

Dear Pa and Ma,

Haven't had time to write lately. We've been hopping about too fast. Heard nothing more about my disturbance. I believe I've got to see the Brigadier sometime. I think they all appreciate as you do, that I'm fighting a different battle. Pardon the publicity, if any, but one can achieve nothing without it. Anyway, I feel happy for the first time for four years, so the chances are I've done the right thing, in spite of the consequences, if any.

I sent an application in to be allowed to go into Boulogne and see the German Cmdr. Sat in my jeep with newly washed pants to serve as a white flag, but permission didn't come!

Waddell's in very good form. Had a letter from Manchester yesterday from some people saying 'Toodleoo'. I have my public apart from Mrs Collingwood – 'But William, it's so shaming for us.'

Not really, Ma, that's what Mr Shaw's mother thought about Bernard.

Love,
WILLIAM

141 R.A.C.,
(The Buffs),
B.L.A.
Sept. 21st, 1944

Dear Pa and Ma,

I saw the Brigadier this morning. He is a very nice man. He said 'I have the greatest respect for anybody who sticks up for their views.' He's sent in a special report saying with my views I am a potential danger to morale and should not be in contact with service men.

I don't think they will let me resign my commission as the report says I have great ability! He thinks I will be sent to look after prisoners of war. Very interesting. My old friend Major Cooper is doing that. It will be much more in my line and should have been done years ago. The Brigadier said 'The trouble is I never took your views seriously. I've always taken my line from the Regiment and treated you as a licensed buffoon!'

What does he think I stood for Parliament three times for? Anyway, the matter seems to be adjusted, except for leaving the regiment – which is very sad.

My French is becoming good, if not perfect. I bought Waddell 100 eggs the other day. I have yet to see one single child who isn't literally bursting with health.

Don't let this episode worry you. It's all turned out O.K. and it's not the soldiers one has to worry about – it's the politicians.

Love,
WILLIAM

141 R.A.C.,
(The Buffs),
B.L.A.
September 26th, [1944]

Dear Pa and Ma,

Thanks very much for letters. I'm delighted that you are unmoved by this episode, or rather that you understand the matter fully. Alec remarked that one couldn't not fight just because one disagreed with Churchill because the war would end. That, of course, is exactly my intention. I've always wanted to know what would happen to someone who did just that. I am in the process of finding out! I have to see the Divisional Commander as soon as we catch up with him.

One of our officers captured a German general the other day. The general remarked that what he didn't know about encirclement wasn't worth knowing. Major Ryle has got the American Silver Star.

There was some rude letter in reply to mine in the Maidenhead paper. I returned them one, and after that, I expect the correspondence will close. Anyway, I've cooked my goose for an English seat, and even the Liberals regard me now with doubting but wistful glances. I can see I shall end up as a Home Rule for Scotland candidate, as I now despair of teaching the English not to be empire-conscious, and if they want independence for small countries, let them have it on their doorstep. Our R.E.M.E. officer comes from Glasgow, and another is a Fife farmer; they are both keen. Waddell doesn't voice his opinion but one could no doubt find him a place harrying the Borderland. I've written one or two poems lately, some of which will appear in *Truth*.

The whole camp is full of Alsatians and cigars taken off the Germans. All the Sqdn. Cmdrs. include looting orders in their plans. The other above-mentioned officer has got the General's pay book, revolver and tablecloth with swastika thereon. The doctor is the most carefree, coming from Ireland as he does. Hoping you're all very well.

Love,
WILLIAM

I had forecast that the affair had blown over, but the situation changed as a result of my writing a letter to the *Maidenhead Advertiser* explaining the whole situation. When this was published, no doubt the Army decided that it had to move.

141 R.A.C.,
The Buffs,
B.L.A.
October 1st, 1944

Dear Pa and Ma,

Thanks very much for letters. I am sorry you have been rung up by the press, but if you refuse to say anything they soon leave one alone. As you say, this publicity is very unpleasant from your point of view, but one can achieve nothing nowadays without it.

I have now been put under arrest, and will doubtless be court martialled, due to that last letter I wrote to the *Maidenhead Advertiser*. I am slightly worried in case those who tried to keep the matter quiet should get into trouble, but I don't see why they should. Short of putting me under arrest, they did all that is required such as relieving me of all duties and reporting me to those above.

I couldn't very well tell the Colonel that I'd written to the paper, because one is not officially allowed to write.

I had a letter from Alec the other day, and one from the Scottish Nationalist, Douglas Young, who is a friend of Jo Grimond's and wears an enormous beard. It was written largely in Latin, which bewildered me somewhat.

Love,
WILLIAM

141. R.A.C.,
(The Buffs),
B.L.A.
October 5th, 1944

Dear Pa and Ma,

Thanks very much for letters. The affair has now reached its inevitable climax. I was court martialled yesterday. The court found me guilty – as indeed they could do nothing else – and I am awaiting the news of the punishment. They are entitled to pop me inside for a while, to turn me out of the

Army. The President was a cute old brigadier covered with medals who used to command our brigade. Two officers from our brigade who were scheduled to be on the court did not turn up and were replaced. I suspect they felt disinclined to sit on it.

Major Edmeades gave a powerful speech in favour of my character, and I made a speech in defence lasting a quarter of an hour emphasising the extenuating circumstances. Captain Westwell, who was my escort and an actor before the war, was miserable because it was the first drama in which he had performed without a speaking part!

I'm very sorry about the publicity and what some people might regard as a stain on the family honour. I hope you don't. Not one officer or man in this regiment has the least inclination – now that one has faced the music – to say that one has done anything in the slightest degree dishonourable. It may be that the court will say something to that effect; on the other hand it is very unlikely that, for political reasons, they can say anything in my favour at all.

You will notice that since the press publicity about the refusal to let civilians out of Le Havre, it has become an established custom at Calais and Dunkirk to do so. Without wishing to flatter myself, that can scarcely be coincidence. The War Office are like a scalded cat, when pricked from behind, and I'll bet a thousand pounds to a click of Collingwood's fingers that they issued a directive on the matter last Friday.

I refrained from saying anything that might get Waddell into trouble, for which he's duly grateful. I'm already getting letters from unknown old ladies congratulating me. There will be lots more.

So drop me a line and let me know that you are not perturbed – apart from the publicity, without which, it is not beyond the bounds of possibility, some of the 18,000 civilians in Calais might have died.

Love,
WILLIAM

264 Delivery Sqdn.,
B.L.A.
Oct. 9th, 1944

Dear Pa and Ma,

I am still awaiting to hear my punishment. I have had no letters lately because post has been delayed everywhere lately. Consequently I do not know your views on this court martial, but I trust it will not unduly disturb you. Not one man in the Buffs had an unpleasant word to say. I realise that it will not be the same among the civil population in England, but had they lived in Calais they might have thought differently. I hope you got my speech for the defence.

The prosecuting officer used to speak for the League of Nations from your platform and sent you his best regards.

Love,
WILLIAM

B.L.A.
Oct. 15th, 1944

Dear Pa and Ma,

Thanks for letters. I was told this morning that I have been cashiered with one year's imprisonment with hard labour. It might have been much, much worse. Please don't let it upset you and don't look upon it as a disgrace. There is no disgrace in breaking the law in what one believes to be a good cause, provided one is prepared to pay the penalty by which the law is upheld – as it must be. Everybody has been remarkably kind to me here. I'll let you know where I go to, and when.

After all, I am not the first person interested in politics who has been prepared to spend a while in jug for sticking to his views. Nor, I hope, shall I be the last. Besides which, it's all good for the character.

Write and tell me you are not too upset, and thank Bridget for her letter.

Love,
WILLIAM

That letter was the last I wrote from France. I wrote the next from Wormwood Scrubs.

The Reluctant Prisoner

[Wormwood Scrubs]
Oct. 24th, 1944

Dear Pa and Ma,

I've arrived at the destination overleaf. They seem to be a little short of ink. I hope you are counted as 'respectable friends'! It seems one is only allowed an occasional letter. It drives me wild. What conceivable satisfaction can anyone get out of stopping a man reading his own letters? Could you get Alec to apply to see me? As an M.P. he should get through. I could then get him to help over my petition to old [Herbert] Morrison which they say replaces an appeal – also he might do something to get letters and newspapers through. After all, I don't read them for my amusement but to keep in touch with one's political life. I should have thought a sentence of hard labour would have forced one to read letters, instead of the reverse. I also find I will have no time for writing a play or book. Instead I shall have to do jobs which require no brain work at all and not much physical. I think I shall apply for a transfer to a country prison where I can go and hack the ground around. Otherwise, I shall go mental – not violent, but a vacant grin and feet pointing backwards.

When I arrived the warder insisted on the Christian name of my next of kin, so you are now down as 'Charles' in the books of W. Scrubs for evermore. The Doctor's orderly told me not to scratch and said 'You are all right.' I gently led him, via my piles, to my nervous system which is very curious and leaves my knees shaking when the air raid warning goes. I'm going to let the doctor have a look at my brain, if he can find it. I was then interviewed by the Padre who wrote briskly on a sheet of paper as he looked due west and murmured in, I think, the tongue of Wales. After that either the Governor or one of his adjutants informed me that the civilians had, in his opinion, been allowed out of Le Havre. With all respect I altered his opinion for him. That's the end of Chapter 1 of 'Peeps at Prison Life'. I hope you are all very well.

Let your reply be of colossal length. Let us have your pound of flesh. It must contain every item of news you have. If they persist in this letter racket, I'll have to get a state-paid secretary. Well, Ma, don't worry about me. I still have my sense of humour – and if old Herbert Morrison has a spark of decency and recalls his idealistic youth before the visions he had were clouded by rich Conservative breath, he should let me out. Looking forward to hearing from you. Alec knew I might ask his assistance. Let anybody who so desires know where I am. Let us have no backstairs diplomacy!

Love to Bridget and Rachel and Henry, etc.

Love,
WILLIAM

Dear Pa and Ma,

No doubt forgetting that the crest of the Honourable Society of Censors is Mr Baldwin's lips (rouge and sealed) dexter to a dragon couchant (Mrs Baldwin), the Deputy Governor informed me that my last letter to you was that of a peevish child. Reading between the lines of the Bible, I judge that there may have been a note of petulance in the first letter that Samson, after chewing up the pillars of the temple, penned to his mamma. As for childishness, it is a pity that I have to change that style, which has ranged from the 'I am quite well. I made 2 yesterday' of 23 years ago to the winged words of recent years – with such success and mutual satisfaction. I tell you this lest you should wonder why the atmosphere of this epistle is like that of Mr Gladstone writing to his creditors.

I have little news for you – only this. If ever the Chancellor of the Exchequer imposes a tax of more than twenty shillings in the pound, please let me know and I will tell you exactly how to open a yale lock with a button and a piece of string. Otherwise, I have grown two beards – the first the kind I understand one used to see King Edward sheltering behind, and the second of the suburban Italian music hall type. The third is at the moment under glass. I have sent in my petition to the Army Council, outlining the difficulty I had in persuading Waddell that although his way of life doubtless suited him, it did not suit me. I also touched lightly, for the benefit of those members of the Army Council who have not done a bit of 'time', on the discrepancy between a military sentence and a civil imprisonment. I recall sending a private soldier to prison once for shooting his friend in the back (by mistake). I trust he went to a detention barracks, otherwise his second barrel will likely be reserved for me. However, all goes well and I cannot complain. I have however asked for a transfer. I hope it will be allowed and I hope it might be to Edinburgh. Then I could get outdoor exercise and you, my dear Mamma, could come to the door disguised as Flora MacDonald and spirit me away beneath your skirt. If you came here and gave the name of F. MacDonald, they would merely say 'Sorry, Madam, 10532 Ramsay MacDonald left in 1917'. I heard rumours, they may or may not be true, that Margaret[1] came the other night at about 8 o'clock and beat herself against the door like a wounded swallow. Anyway, she was sent away, if she came, and rightly. We retire early here. On the question of letters, I think you are only allowed to write in *reply* to mine, once fortnightly. Of course, if something profound occurred like an Armistice or if Lord William Scott[2] was asked to form a government, you could then write and the Governor would inform me that a miracle had taken place.

I shall have to appoint Bridget as my secretary. Here are the divers laws and ordinances for her perusal. (1) She is to open all my letters and, so far as private letters are concerned, she is to make a list of writers and a resumé of the sentiments

[1] My sister-in-law, then married to my brother Henry.
[2] My brother-in-law, married to my sister Rachel.

expressed therein. The only snag in this department is likely to be my friend Robin Fyfe, now in the Grenadiers, and once in the Indian Army. He spent a lot of time with the Afghans, fell on his head twice playing polo, and now writes stories for, I think, *Chambers' Magazine*. Unfortunately, those stories which Chambers, quite rightly, rejects, he sends to me. They and the expressions he uses in his letters – typed by a long-suffering wife – are the kind of literature which I imagine is not touched on in the Afghan world until late in the evening when the squaws have gone upstairs into the drawing room. Treat those as your mother treats a mushroom. Otherwise, you are answerable for what you read yourself and I expect you to conform to the motto of the Censor College, 'Trappist Monks are chatterboxes'. (2) All public and political letters you will answer as follows. If friendly: 'My brother, who is in W. Scrubs, thanks you and looks forward to replying when he comes out.' If unfriendly: 'My brother, who is in prison, notes your remarks and looks forward to pushing your face in when . . . ' Make a list of names and forward in Pa's letter or Ma's. (Also answer private ones.) (3) Write to Major R. Edmeades in my regiment (same address). Give him my love, ask for news, ask him to tell Captain Westwell that 'The Offending Adam'[1] is in its birth pangs and to warn the doctor against too much drink. He must of course write back to you. (4) Write to Andrew McLaren M.P. and ask him to apply to Morrison to see me. Also Dennis Kendall, M.P. He's tough but useful.

Alec was very helpful. I want him to chase up that petition and not let the Army Council go to bed with it. Regarding Conscientious Objector, I have decided against it. Please write to Miss Nancy Browne, 6 Endsleigh St., London WC1, thank for letter, but I do not mean to apply. Point out in your own words that I am glad I was misinformed in 1940 because I've had an unforgettable experience, that I lack the courage to be a C.O., that, having been punished, I cannot hide behind my conscience. I am no saint. It makes me laugh

[1] Title for a projected play.

sardonically to think that I, who have run wild and unhindered, and broken most of the commandments, should be imprisoned for refusing to break the sixth. Tell Alec to abandon the tribunal idea. My position is clear. I have gone against my conscience in the past if I thought it the most intelligent thing to do. It is not so spotless that I can use it for a shield. Far from it. It has one or two particularly nasty dents in it, and to hide behind its dented armour would be laughable. It so happens that what I did at Le Havre my conscience agrees with, but that is not the point. The point is that I am a political objector, that I say, and shall continue to say, that this war has exceeded its playing time. I don't put Mr Churchill's conscience in the witness box. I assume he's doing his best and I think he's wrong. I ask the same treatment in return, and refuse to be labelled and put aside as what the world wrongly regards as a crank. I could be just as good a soldier as the Duke of Marlborough (past not present) but I am not a soldier, and I entirely disapprove of the modern D. of Marlborough's war. It is my object to teach people, however inadequately, that soldiers have minds of their own. Consciences are private affairs, and I will not have mine vetted by some seedy old knight who sold the troops marmalade in the Crimean War. Sorry, that's used up all the paper. Unless somebody does what I'm doing, all the children of Robin's[1] age will grow up with the idea that, unless you shoot somebody every morning in the tube with a tommy gun, you're not entitled to your first eleven colours.

Love,
WILLIAM

[Wormwood Scrubs]

Dear Pa and Ma,

I'm afraid this nib is past active service, so I'll have to write in ink after all. Strange to relate, I'm now getting used to the

[1] My brother Henry's elder son.

dear old place. However, I hope to get my transfer; the exercise problem is acute and the monotony and getting used to a prison is the thing I dread. I'm keeping well; had a slight cold, largely due to the fact that the exercise boulevard here is paved with two or three inches of water in inclement weather.

Thanks very much for that gigantic letter. Did you take a couple of days in bed after it? I understand it is O.K. for you both and Bridget to write a letter each on the same piece of foolscap, if you follow me. Then nobody need exhaust themselves and her report on my correspondence can be written by herself. I'm extremely disturbed about this letter from Bill. How could I know who it was? It might be Bill Crandall, or Sir William Beveridge or the Adjutant in my regiment. What did it say? Was the writing like Chinese? I grow more and more irritated with a Government restriction which leaves one for a fortnight to wonder which of one's friends has been wounded. Mrs Beesley, who wrote from California, is Dodie Smith; she married her manager just after *Bonnet over the Windmill,* doubtless written to warm the cockles of his heart.

I am hoping to get Margaret to call in the next day or two. A major in the Parachute Corps called on Saturday and said some very charming things about the activity that brought me here. I thought for a while he was a spy or a secret service agent and expected him, at any moment, to slip a poisoned cigarette across the table, or alternatively to mutter a few words to the tune of an Arabic song describing the layout of an aerodrome 3,000 feet above sea level on the Afghan frontier. Instead he told me he was writing a book.

I have at last got an idea for a literary work which I hope will be no. 3 vol. to *Gulliver's Travels* and *Alice in Wonderland*. I intend to write it so that any of my nephews and nieces can understand every word of it, because the things that they can understand are the only things worth understanding. For those who care to seek the hidden meaning, there will not be disappointment. I only hope that if and when I get a transfer, the facilities for literary creation will be greater than they are here, where the only man who is allowed to follow his own profession is the hair cutter. On second thoughts, I can see the difficulties which would inevitably result from an attempt to allow the majority to follow their professions.

There is a very nice youth from Ayr here, who used to work on the railway around Lanark and Carstairs. He's been in the Navy for four years and is only twenty-two. His comments on the people of Glasgow and Edinburgh make me laugh a good deal, and his grandmother is a keen Scottish Nationalist who emphasises her arguments with her umbrella. It is more and more forced upon my notice how delightful it is when you can talk about politics, as you can to a Scotchman, without any personal element entering into it, in a purely objective way. Unlike Englishmen, they have self-confidence instead of pride.

Could you ask Bridget to write to Jakie Astor and congratulate him on his marriage. Tell him I am unable to send him a wedding present as the purchase tax is too high around here, but I could let him have either a mailbag (hand woven) or a brown canvas belt, both my own personal work. By the way, my income tax form arrived here from the Travellers' Club the other day and opposite 'Present Employment' I wrote the most facetious comments and I believe it's gone back. I can picture the civil service official who receives it at his desk there in Caernarvonshire dropping it into the waste paper basket as though it were a dead mouse. Also could we find out from Mr Pinker, my agent at Clay Cross, what he did with my suits (and suitcases) and if he's got receipts from the railway for them. If he's wearing them himself, ask him to have them pressed and returned to above address.

Presumably the war is still going on. I have heard it whispered in the corners of the prison that at the Mansion House lunch Mr Churchill sounded as though he'd had a drop too much lemonade.

Could Bridget also write to Mrs Davies, Ellisdene, Taplow, Bucks, thank her for her kind words in the past and ask her to confirm my opinion that my activities have finished me as a politician in the Maidenhead area for good. She's the wife of an officer in my regt. Tell her I last saw him in a café in a Belgian village with a glass of cognac in his hand and I believe he's there still. I doubt if the cognac is.

I want to know these things because my future political career, which the purblind regard as concluded, could either take place in Windsor or Glasgow. If my name stinks (as the Bible has it) in Maidenhead, then it would be politic (which, for once, means intelligent) to go back to Glasgow where my term of imprisonment will merely serve to draw me nearer to my audience, and where I find the people far more friendly, with their eyesight focused somewhat further than the middle foreground – which is Windsor maximum. (Although I have a soft spot in the heart for Maidenhead.)

Love,
WILLIAM

[Wormwood Scrubs]

My dear Pa and Ma,

You were quite right about the letter question. You are only allowed to write *in answer* to my letter. Therefore, the letter of yours I got yesterday was really the answer to *this* one! Consequently, I shall not expect to hear from you until you reply to the one I will write in a fortnight's time. Is that clear as Mr Churchill's war aims? It's my fault for telling you to write independently, when I first got here, and thought that the censorship regulations might prove intolerable.

With regard to your visit, my dear Papa, the same advice applies to you. If you are in this area, yes. But if not, is it worth it? However, I am told I shall shortly be transferred to the camp, which is an annexe to the prison in the country, where there are no walls and a large area in which one can walk, and woods and birds' nests and delightful scenery. So, I should come there when the weather is better.

I am allowed one visit ½ hr. per fortnight, and 1 hr. per month. The whole method of arranging for and organising for a visit is so involved and bureaucratic as to drive me into a state of irritable impotence, which is the first sign of prison-rot. Anything so simple as allowing somebody to write and say 'Is it O.K. for me to visit you on such and such a date?' and allowing one to answer 'Yes' or in certain circumstances 'No', has yet to burst like a flash of divine fire on the minds of the prison reformers.

This letter is really granted so that I can ask you to send me £1 (one pound) to pay a dentist who pulled out a tooth for me last week. He won't require it all. It was a very bad tooth and had the beginning of an abscess on the end. The doctor was prepared to let it go till June, but I'm glad to say the dentist removed it.

The Army Council sent their regrets about my petition. Very disappointing, especially, the insistence on the 'cashiering'. I'll try one more in which I shall try to point out that it's a little hard to be thrown out in disgrace, having tried to be relieved of one's commission without success.

Their argument, no doubt, is that one can't resign one's commission in the field. Yet private soldiers can be imprisoned for years without *any ignominy or disgrace* for mutiny or refusing to obey an order. Why not an officer?

Love,
WILLIAM

My petition for a transfer to Edinburgh was turned down by the Home Office and a compromise arrived at through a transfer to Wakefield Prison.

I was driven from Wormwood Scrubs to King's Cross handcuffed to a prison officer where we both boarded the train, still handcuffed together – a situation which was just tolerable when seated in the railway carriage but became less comfortable in certain other circumstances. And so we came to Wakefield.

[Wakefield Prison]
8.12.44

Dear Pa and Ma,

As you will observe, my request to be transferred has brought me here. There is less solitude – for example, one messes in a party of a dozen or so. I thank my stars for my early theatrical days and for the fact that my politics persuaded me to become a conscripted private soldier, because such things made a sudden transformation of this nature quite innocuous. I have reached the conclusion that the worst thing about prison life is the fact that one is under observation all the time. Were it not that my literary training has enabled me to adopt a system of counter-observation, I should find it quite intolerable. It inevitably means that one's existence becomes a humiliating ride on horseback through the streets of Coventry. Whereas in the Army, on occasions when that ride has to be overlooked, it is done with tact and decorum from behind closed shutters; there is at least the illusion of privacy. In my two months sojourn as His Majesty's guest, I have, *au contraire*, found the route lined by numerous well-meaning citizens. That means that Lady Godiva, deprived of her last shred of privacy, must inevitably become one of these two things in order to complete her journey, namely, brazen or introspective underneath a cloak. Both of these conditions are, I think I'm right in saying, fundamentally unsound.

Do you know the story of the Frenchman who, when asked if he had dined on the boat, replied 'Au contraire'?

I am helping to produce *The Babes in the Wood* for Xmas. I have got a sketch from H.M. Tennent's to do as well. I shall need to appear as an Indian Army Officer of uncertain age. Could you send my service tunic here (as many pips as you can find), service trousers, a topee (or any military hat, but I've seen one in the Long Room) and a row or two of medals. I don't mind if they're the ribbons or gongs. Army shirt and tie. And two cigars, or four – two for dress rehearsal. It would be helpful if you could duplicate any of these things because two

Indian Army officers are required. I hesitate to ask for those red tabs you wear on your uniform, but if Collingwood could produce any material of the same colour it would be delightful.

I see Mr Churchill has asked for a vote of confidence again. He'll try that game once too often.

I have read the bible up to Isaiah so far. Good reading, and some shocking old rascals I had forgotten about.

Love,
WILLIAM

[Wakefield Prison]

Dear Pa and Ma,

I have now discovered that visits don't take place on Sundays, which is evidently written on the visiting card, which of course one does not see. It is evidently part of the system devised to bring home to one the fact that ignorance of the law is no excuse for breaking it. I have also discovered that those who come on Saturdays are doing the popular thing. Consequently, you may well find that when you shout across the table to me 'How are you?' Mrs Brown from Middlesbrough may reply 'All right love, except for me kidneys.'

Except for people throwing tobacco tins and the usual show of knives, the atmosphere is like the bower in Dundock on a moonlit night. The prospect of a visit in the great open spaces is now not to be. The doctor decided that I was not to go to Camp. In a charitable mood, one would say that he had decided that the work there was too heavy for me. In a critical mood, that he was an agent of the Conservative Central Office with orders to keep me under lock and key until the General Election. Whatever the cause – and let us say it was the former – you need have no fears that it was due to any failing in my health. I am still on my wood-stacking party, and my health is O.K. It has improved vastly since the days of Wormwood Scrubs, when the sound of the air-raid siren turned my stomach over like an acrobat at Bertram Mills's Circus. It still turns over at any untoward noise, such as a railway engine snorting in the night, but with more gentle convulsions. In other words, I have come to the conclusion that I want a rest. In that, if not in all else, I am at one with every soldier and civilian who has lived in this country since 1939. It is, of course, useless to imagine that prison is a rest, because one cannot rest in a vacuum. What you were when you came in, broadly speaking, you are when you go out. Nor can the brain, which, in my case, must be active to be healthy, function in prison. That is why, apart from producing pretentious uninspiring histories, no monk, out of contact with the world in a monastery, has ever penned what Mr Matthew Arnold calls 'a spark from Heaven,' on the written page. No man can become good at tennis if there is nobody across the net to hit him back the ball.

However, I've been reading a lot. I have only three books of the Bible left to read. I read *Antony* by Lord Lytton last night. And I am still assaulting Dr Johnson. Burns's poems I find very good. I shudder to think that I dared to stand for Parliament in Scotland without knowing any of them. However, I find I share his views. That is the time to read, when one knows what one's views are. Ask Alec to send me *Hansard* of this debate about Yalta. I expect he will speak about Poland. He seems, if I mistake me not, a trifle indignant about the treatment Poland is getting. Not the first man who has been so in the last 500 years. He is of course displeased that Mr Churchill should say 'No' to Germany and 'Yes' to Russia. I am with him there, but I am not with him if – as I suspect – he has a suppressed feeling that we should say 'No' to both. Let him consider such things nearer home, and ask himself 'Imperialism of any brand, or not?' If the answer is yes, then it is yes to Russia *and* to Germany. If it is no, then I agree that it is no to both. But it is no to Britain, too. 'But we haven't got an empire, William.' 'Nor has Russia, it's a union of Soviet Republics.' That will be enough politics. Hoping you are all very well. And let me know what you think about a visit next month. Or will I get a transfer o'er the Border?

Love,

WILLIAM

[Wakefield Prison]

Dear Pa and Ma,

Thanks very much for books. Unfortunately the mailbag situation here is so acute that it effectually quenches any intellectual enlightenment. It's a pity, because there's quite a good library here, which might as well be stacked with canvas, wax and thread. Before Christmas I was excused them, being on the concert, and got a lot of reading done.

The last book I managed to read had the following description of Mr Gladstone's Parliament in 1883. 'The Speaker had called on the young man with the sallow complexion and the coal-black hair, and did not seem inclined to abandon anything of his just privilege. The day had come, and here was the man, with his hands resting on his hips, and his eyes wandering over the uproarious assembly. He was evidently nervous, having, possibly, sometimes dreamed of making his maiden speech, but not reckoning it would be delivered in these circumstances, and would be of the particular kind he now had in mind. As the House would not cease its uproar, he thought he had better begin. So with hands awkwardly disposed on his hips, and his head restlessly moving from side to side, he got out a few sentences. These, catching the ear of the House amid the turmoil, turned out to be very brave words indeed, and presently he had the House quiet and listening. He had been hurt by the haughty tone of the Premier and now gave back defiance in response to command. "If the Government won't carry out the wishes of the majority," he said, with as much apparent unconcern as if he were considering whether he should call a hansom or a four-wheeler, "it would be easy to obtain another Government that will."'

Who was it, my dear Mamma? The first sentence of the chapter will provide the clue. '"Le Jour Viendra" is the motto of the House of Durham and at the stroke of six o'clock this afternoon (July 9th) it occurred to the Honourable Frederick Lambton[1] that it had come.'

You see, I get all my characteristics which lead me into trouble from the distaff side! My aversion from obstinate dictatorial Prime Ministers from my grandfather, and my deep affection for the racecourse from your Uncle Jack.[2] As the chronicler remarked, 'It is a bad sign for a leader when Liberals of historic name and tried fidelity speak thus, and Mr Lambton's remarkable deliverance only too surely presaged the disaster that followed in the division lobby.' Encore, I say, encore!

I have been out two days last week on a 'wood party' on a high hill in the snow. It was delightful and the fresh air was like a dram or two of whisky. I trust the custom will be regular shortly. I saw two duck, a magpie or two, and made friends with a robin which looked a trifle chilly and could clearly do with a pair of prison boots.

If you could call when you are at York, it would be delightful. But, don't if it's inconvenient. If you can, I suggest you give the Governor a tinkle on the blower and ask him if you can adjust the hours of visiting to suit your meetings. They are very accommodating here. Don't forget, before you come, to stuff your bowler hat with sweets, tobacco, files, jemmies and the like, which you will have to pass to me by sleight of hand across a wide, four-foot, highly polished table under the keen eye of a warder armed with a huge club and a case of poisoned darts. It would be as well to practise it before you come, bearing in mind the fact that if your performance is at all imperfect, the sufferer will be myself. You will be able to get away with it by explaining that you are a professional conjuror.

I have written a petition to Mr Morrison in verse. I am

[1] Mother's father.
[2] Lord Durham.

sending it this week. If it does nothing else, I feel it may produce a smile. A letter from Lady Astor last week. She says she's coming to see me in Feb. It rests with the authorities of course, but personally I wouldn't let her into a prison except to stay, or else in chains. She's a sweet old thing, and wrote a delightful letter. You can bring two hangers-on when you visit, if you like.

The Chaplain in chapel this morning, meaning to say 'Everywhere are footprints and a finger pointing, etc', said 'Everywhere there are finger prints.' Highly topical and well-received remark. Hoping you are all well.

Love,
WILLIAM

[Wakefield Prison]

Dear Pa and Ma,

I went to see the doctor this morning, my nervous system being out of order. He made me give a résumé of all my activities since about 1930, and when he asked about one year and I said I was in Germany or Spain, and then two years later I was on the stage, he had me back and asked what I was doing in between. I have an idea he was pulling my leg. Still, it's a stimulating change to have that process reversed for once.

I was talking to a man here the other day about Oxford and mentioned that I got sent down twice. He said 'I was sent down from Oxford, too. Three years from Mr Justice Charles.'

I read a sentence or two from Alec's speech in one paper. He seemed to talk sense. Of course I've always said the young fellow had a future for himself in politics if only he could avoid becoming too feudal. I'm expecting those *Hansards*. I approve of Mr Strauss resigning. I don't entirely approve of his reasons, but the gesture is encouraging. Far too many politicians say to themselves, 'I entirely disagree with this or that, but it would not be in the public interest for me to resign.' How wrong they are. The effect on their own reputations could be only healthy. In future, when Mr Strauss holds an opinion one will know he holds it because he really holds it, and not because somebody wants him to.

It'll be O.K. to answer this when received. If you think it is in order, could you drop a line to Marten and congratulate him on being made Provost.[1] Tell him I clearly remember when leaving Eton I asked him what I should do and he said 'Politics', and point out that even here, in this cold and sordid cell, I think that he was right!

Love,
WILLIAM

[Wakefield Prison]
1st Jan., 1945

Dear Pa and Ma,

The Christmas concert went off well. I did not perform personally as the Lord Chamberlain's writ does not run inside a prison, and my contribution was considered near the edge. However I said a few words at the end on behalf of my fellow crooks, and the Governor replied more or less to the effect that the nauseous impression I had created had been somewhat mitigated by the soothing hand of time! In fact, a good Christmas and a dose of bicarbonate of soda was had by all. I have now disposed of Mr Asquith, almost of Cobden of the firm of Cobden and Bright, and next week I'm being acquainted with Mr Balfour.

The whole of Lord Oxford's notes and letters are studded with little comments like 'Winston very gay and bellicose', 'Winston all for a show-down', 'Winston hears the trumpet call'. I have no doubt if his nurse's memoirs were available they would read 'Winston needs a good slapping, but Her Ladyship said "no"'.

My literary activities are rather interrupted by the mail-bags which appear from time to time in my cell. I did not

[1] C. H. K. Marten, Provost of Eton.

notice the earthquake the other night, though some of my colleagues reported a rather tepid attempt by a supernatural force to unlock their doors and let them free. My petition has been away nearly two months now. I'll let you know if there's any prospect of a move. I think I'll have to wait until the return of my petition first. I do not anticipate a satisfactory outcome to this petition but, on legal grounds, they ought really to reconsider the sentence.

I did no harm to old Waddell by mentioning the letters I had plied him with, because he had already been relieved of his command, and it was only to avoid that very thing that I withheld them at the Court Martial. It amazed me to hear that he had been removed. How Maj. Gen. Hobart, my Divisional Commander, could confirm my sentence with one hand, as it were, and sack Herbert with the other, I can't conceive. It must be nearly the first time in military history that the prosecuting and defending officers have been punished for the same offence.

I see Mr Eden has conceived an idea to give Danzig to the Poles. If he gave his grandmother to George Robey it would contribute more (in the negative sense) to the future peace of Europe. The only reasons he could put forward for giving it to Poland are (1) that it is 99% German (2) that the Russians might one day ask for it, and (3) that the Poles do not want it. In my judgement, those reasons are inadequate. However, he will doubtless do it. I feel like I have felt standing in the wings of a theatre towards the end of an act, watching some moon-faced stage hand preparing to set the stage again for Act III.

Love,
WILLIAM

[Wakefield Prison]
[December 1944]

Dear Pa and Ma,

Are any of you contemplating a visit? Much as I should like

to see you, I would scarcely advise it. It's a long way to spend half an hour on the opposite side of a ping-pong table without a ping-pong bat. In any case, perhaps in a month or two, like some swallow rested on a telegraph wire, I'll continue my migration north. Happy Christmas to you all. It seems that there are very reasonable festivities here. Not mixed, of course. One hears some prize things in joints like this. During a political argument a man said, 'Don't waste any time talking about Liberals and Labour and Communists. I'm a Conservative, my job depends on it.' When asked his job, he was of course a burglar. (Alec might try that as a slogan at the next election. I've often wondered where the Conservative majority came from.) The best of all was perpetrated by our youth from Lanark. Having received a letter or information to the effect that his young lady had been walking out elsewhere, and being at a loss how to deal with the situation, he took down the library book in his cell called *Love Letters of History*, selected one written in petulant mood by Nelson to Lady Hamilton, copied it down verbatim on the staid prison writing paper, affixed his signature and sent it off. I have yet to hear the sequel, but what a perfect example of the continuity of British naval tradition.

I am now reading a gigantic *Life of Asquith*. It informs me that when he burst into tears in the House one day, Tim Healey remarked 'This is the greatest miracle in the history of the world since Moses struck the rock.' Could you get me Hal Fisher's *History of England*? That gigantic piece, whose creation I so frequently interrupted on the occasions when he sent me down. I intend to read that, then embark on the autobiographies of all the more interesting boys. By that means I shall keep my brain manured, although uncultivated.

Dear Bridget, pull up your slacks! There will be many normal people, with relations killed or for other reasons, who will regard me unavoidably with much distaste. Who are they? In Alec's last letter to me, in Belgium, he said he was worried by people like me being prepared to compromise with evil. I had no time to inform him that I was not primarily concerned with evil and – this is the point – that I was equally worried by His Majesty's Government refusal, so far as Germany's concerned, to compromise with what little good there may be there. Even assuming we are 99% right and 1% wrong and Germany is 99% wrong and 1% right, unconditional surrender is unjustifiable because it refuses to compromise with that 1% of right. If he argues, hit him with a mustard-seed.

It is Sunday today, I have a heavy cold. It is no use going to the doctor, because prison law, which shelters as it were on Sinai, in deep impenetrable darkness, would doubtless deny him the urge to treat me with a double Scotch. I prefer to let it run its harmless course. Could you send me a very cheap pipe. By the 8th. Jan. I shall have earned in my prison life sufficient money – to wit 1/1½d – to buy ½ oz. of a substance which, for want of any other suitable name, is called tobacco.

I have some stimulating political arguments. There are a few of the boys here who regard themselves as Communists. I join issue with them on the question of whether what takes place in Russia is what they think it is, and endeavour to ease their future susceptibilities by warning them that in five years' time Uncle Joe may be giving a very passable imitation of Peter the Great. I have no quarrel with Communists, in fact I might well be one myself were it not for the fact that, in their arrogance, they brook no opposition. Far be it from me to force other people to emulate my own activities. I see no enjoyment in a political life without opposition, it's like playing tennis against a wall, because you've smashed up your opponent, in a temper, with your racket. It is – the Communist Party, at the moment – Christianity without humility, or tolerance, or understanding, or a sense of humour. In other words it wants to adjust its dress before it goes out courting.

The Chaplain here is a very good preacher. Admittedly he lacks the violence of the Rev. Davies, but there is no reason to suppose clear thought can only be achieved in a high wind.

My petition is still out. I shall shortly be sending a petition to H. Morrison, embodying my New Year's Greetings and one or two other little points. I grow very hungry here in the evenings. Bread and butter and cocoa just before five and then Mrs Pankhurst in a Government-controlled hunger strike. One could of course take up food from the daytime meals to one's cell. However, I dread that habit following me into private life. One's hostess might reasonably regard it as a reflection on her household management.

Love,

WILLIAM

[Wakefield Prison]

28.1.45

Dear Pa and Ma,

That letter to which Bridget refers is from Staff-Sgt. UTTING, Royal Tank Corps. His name is Jack, his wife's name Jacqueline, and his dog's Caesar. He was an instructor at Bovington, used to live in a caravan near the camp, and when the School greatly expanded in 1941 and the R.S.M. called 'Right markers, open to 200 paces!' is alleged to have reached his position at the end of the queue on a bicycle. Thank him for his letter, please.

There's a lot of snow here. My life is of the kind that you would strongly approve, my dear Mamma. I rise about 6.30, have porridge and tea for breakfast and bread, go out at 8 to the top of a high hill, where the air is 100% vitamins, and work at stacking timber (very congenial and not too heavy), return at 5.30, hot meal at 6.15, bed at 7.30. Four cigarettes a day and no alcohol has passed my lips since I landed at Northolt aerodrome! The result is that whereas, when I was in the prison all day, an influenza germ with one arm and a wooden leg could have knocked me down for the count, I now have biceps like Carnera and a flush on the cheek like Lady Cunard after a visit to the beauty specialist. I have come to the conclusion that there is something rather restful about prison. Here, as nowhere else in the world, everybody is known for what they are and their individual weakness is no secret. Consequently, by a strange paradox everything is open, if not above board. How salutary if that were so in ordinary life. If, for example, a man who tried to sell one something had on his identity card 'Apt to charge double the price', or a man who introduced one to his wife, had a label in his button hole 'Normally has two', or a man who stopped you on a dark night and asked for your purse, was designated 'Liable to use a razor other than for shaving' – how much simpler life would be. I have reached the conclusion that everybody in or out of prison has a private weakness, or sin, and that all passports, identity cards, etc., should have after 'Personal no., colour of eyes, height, etc.' a space for 'Personal Sin'.

The Army Council still haven't answered my petition. And the time is now greatly in excess of their normal period. Does it mean that they are pondering over it, or merely that some absent-minded general has long ago employed my plea to light his pipe? I now realise, looking back on my Army career, that I should have avoided this impasse by pulling a few strings and landing myself a nice job like R.T.O. at Cornhill. It was my obstinate refusal to volunteer for another job – or indeed any job – which forbade me to make an official application for a transfer, even though I dropped hints which would have pierced the hide of a mentally undeveloped rhinoceros. However, doubtless in the long run I shall appreciate the value of having left the strings alone.

We are hoping to do *Young England* for the Easter play and have sent for the copies thereof.

Love,
WILLIAM

[Wakefield Prison]

Dear Pa and Ma,

We have the concert tomorrow. Several of the choicest

items have been censored at the last minute. State institutions have never taken very kindly to burlesque. Those uniforms will come in useful and I'll get permission to send them back next week as well as any books I am allowed to keep.

I had a letter from the Liberal Association informing me that they were sorry they could not consider me a candidate. Actually, I believe they were genuinely sorry, having been enamoured of me in the past. As I thought, they would regard my presence as an embarrassment.

I thought de Valera answered Mr Churchill's sabre-rattling in a very dignified way, which made the latter look a little like a rude boy reproved by a tutor. He also made a shrewd reference to Chamberlain, because he knows full well that his policy, once the drum-beating and excitement of war is gone, is far nearer the true feelings of the British people than Churchill's ever was or ever will be. Now that the appeasement accusation is all square since Yalta, there remains the fact that, assuming one follows the traditional Conservative foreign policy, Churchill is a quarrelsome exponent thereof, while Chamberlain was not. And quarrelsome people invariably finish up by quarrelling.

Love,
WILLIAM

[Wakefield Prison]
April 9th, 1945

Dear Pa and Ma,

The concert went off very well. The boys in the play were a bit slow, but good, and didn't forget their lines. My Dance of the Seven Mailbags was very heavy going to begin with. I had seven wound round my torso, but when I had discarded them one by one with my back to the audience, I did some exotic dancing and then swung round, throwing wide my cloak (a mailbag) – revealing a pair of red drawers and the usual offices over the chest. They say nothing so exotic has been seen since Cleopatra's day.

I sent in a portentous petition to the Army Council in an endeavour to get off being cashiered. I doubt if they'll consider it. Conventional action is what they have to judge one by – at least, they don't have to, but they nearly always do. They shouldn't however confuse an inevitable punishment (i.e. imprisonment) with an optional insult added (i.e. cashiering). It would be a heckler's paradise at a political meeting for me to arrive calling myself the Hon. William having been dishonoured in the Army. It would surely be a case of 'his honour rooted in dishonour stood'! I think I shall have to allow that adjunct to my name to lapse, thus removing the tomato from the hand of the heckler. However, I have yet to hear the Army Council's verdict. Perhaps, like Brutus after his unfortunate lapse at the Capitol, I find myself restored.

We had a very High Church priest functioning this morning in the Padre's absence on holiday. After all the outward and visible show, I was interested to see him going out afterward in a pair of grey plus-fours, thus showing an inward attire worthy of Mr Bernard Shaw.

Now that the concert is over, the usual run of boredom has commenced again. There is another shortly, but we haven't started rehearsing yet.

The expression people use when the end of one's sentence is approaching is 'Is it dragging?' They scratch off the days one by one on little almanacs, thus making everything twice as long. I learnt not to do that at Eton! As Evelyn Waugh so rightly says, 'Any man who has been to an English public school will feel very much at home in prison.'

Love,

WILLIAM

[Wakefield Prison]
23.4.45

Dear Pa and Ma,

I have my usual weekend cold. After our Saturday morning

bath we sit in a corridor in which the draught resembles nothing so much as the slipstream of a Spitfire.

The Chaplain in his sermon this morning remarked that imprisonment made people unnaturally introspective. What a terrific condemnation of imprisonment, that people should be put in an environment which forces them into the particular state of mind which leads to selfishness and anti-social conduct.

Love,
WILLIAM

[Wakefield Prison]
– May 1945

Dear Pa and Ma,

Thanks very much for letter. I have no news except that I've had to replace my vest. The weather has been terribly cold, and those trees and flowers which were deceived by the heat wave must now be regretting their impetuosity. Outside in the great big world my occasional glimpses of the papers inform me that the war in the West is as good as over. It is great news, and if one deserves a punishment, one is getting it now, being immured in this dump at such a moment. However, there are many who contributed somewhat more than I did to the victory, who have gone beyond the world of wars and prisons to a world – I trust – with neither. It makes me a little sick to see so many of my colleagues concerned solely with the prospect of an early release for themselves. However, had I a long time to do I would probably feel the same. Incidentally, I find my release is dated the 5th [June] rather than the 6th. I must have mistaken it in the first and only moment when I looked at it at Wormwood Scrubs.

Alec mentioned something about a job and whether he could do anything. However, I am still at the disposal of Mr Bevin and he will doubtless call me up for some form of National Service until my age group is released, which should not be long. I trust he will permit a month's holiday first.

Then there is the question of the General Election. If I can afford it – in fact even if I can't – I must partake in that. I cannot retire from the political scene merely in view of the fact that I will almost inevitably be beaten. And what is more, I must get started at once. I think it might be best if I went to London for two days on my exit from here and saw the Liberal Association and got a straight answer, yes or no, from them as to whether they want me or whether they have – as the Americans say – had me. So far as Windsor is concerned I would not stand against another Liberal if there is one, nor would I stand if all my 7,000 supporters have deserted me or (if you like) imagine that I have deserted them. But if there is any support of a few faithful henchmen, I must try it again – if only once. The alternative is Scotland and it is possible the Liberals might decide that tucked away in Scotland my presence in their ranks might not stain their 1945 escutcheon, and that perhaps when the gale of war is still, I might add lustre to it later on. That is why I say it might be better to go to London for two days and get this settled because without it, my holiday at Hirsel, to which I look forward, will not provide that rest which a settled prospect of the future can supply.

You will doubtless agree that I cannot afford to stand down for fear of being beaten – even if it might appear more intelligent to do so.

So far as the financial situation is concerned, I must try and get it from the party or from supporters. Having got into Parliament, I shall be able to keep the bailiffs out. Having failed, I should now be able to get a good job in journalism – at least I hope so. And if the Liberals kick me in the pants, there are other parties. I regard all the left-wing parties in England as Whigs, and, though the Liberals are the purest bred, they are not the only branch of the family. Once this ridiculous and misleading class war is resolved, out of which the Labour Party was quite illegitimately born, it should be possible for all the boys to get together to resume the battle of Whigs and Tories, when they discussed politics and not whether one man had an Oxford accent and the other one wore bicycle clips. Political opinions should not be side-tracked into discussions of that kind. Whether a Communist or a Tzarist nobleman sits in Warsaw it is still Polish and – what Lord Dunglass is apt to overlook! – whether an English prince or a lance-corporal member of the Whig Labour Party stands on Gibraltar, it is still a rocky promontory of the Spanish mainland. Many happy returns to Bridget for Fri.

Love,
WILLIAM

[Wakefield Prison]
[May 1945]

Dear Ma and Pa,

There is no danger of my being like Oswald Mosley, because I am democratic. I am not a rebel or a revolutionary, except in war, when democracy was, in my view, unnecessarily suspended. Now that there is freedom again I have no quarrel with anyone. I only want like everybody else to put my point of view, which I regard as urgent and without which I have really very little right to be alive. Furthermore, my political views are just as responsible and only slightly removed say from Alec's or any Conservative for whose opinions I entertain the respect that they deserve.

I honestly feel that my career which has been placed in jeopardy through my own fault, will be conclusively finished, if I fail to face this challenge. I feel that in my deepest instinct, and I know that it is right.

Now to deal with the chance of winning. Naturally you find it hard to believe that in, say, Windsor, nearly 7,000 people take one of your younger children seriously. They voted for me in the dangerous days and were only restrained from voting for me en masse by the pressure of the Coalition and the war situation, both of which are now removed. The only obstacle now is imprisonment, which from information I have received does not deter a lot of people from supporting me still. They are at one with me in feeling that a new spirit and a humanising of politics is the only chance of making this second war worth while. And so for that matter are you. I cannot refuse to centralise their views in myself except on financial grounds.

Love,
WILLIAM

Shortly after I had written that letter, my parents came to see me – in the ping-pong table room, as I had forecast. When they left (my mother wrote and told me later), she had got into the taxi at the gate, only to see my father walking down outside the prison wall towards a big house. 'Where're you going, Charlie?' she called. 'Hold on, Lil,' he called back, 'I'm just going along to thank the dear little Governor for having William here.'

[Wakefield Prison]

Dear Pa and Ma,

It was delightful seeing you yesterday. You will now realise what I mean when I talk of the awkwardness of prison visits. However much one tries, it is impossible to talk about anything but trivial things. First of all the time is too short and one spends all one's time trying to remember the things one wanted to say, and, secondly, the shock of seeing people one knows after months of confinement is too great to be overcome in half an hour. That is why when a soldier or anyone else returns home from a long absence the first thing he does is to sink into a chair and let the full enjoyment come over him gradually, and speaks when the spirit moves him. Nor, when meeting his parents for the first time for a year and a half, does he go out into the street and ask the first policeman he sees to come and share the moment, however charming the policeman may be in private life.

The prison commissioners still think otherwise, and endeavour to force into half an hour a social and emotional interlude which cannot be so treated. And if ever I get onto the prison reform committees, I shall emphasise the need for studying the mental processes of prisoners, and shall display from my own experience the shock any home or family influence has on a prisoner by telling the unbelieving that when I got your first letter and saw it lying on the table in my cell, believe it or not, the tears streamed down my face onto a portion of the floor in Wormwood Scrubs. Had the officer looked through the peephole in that door at that moment, he would doubtless have thought I was washing down my cell.

Love,
WILLIAM

H.M. Prison,
Wakefield
12.6.45

Dear Lord Home,

I am much obliged to you for your kind letter of the 9th instant. Your son left here in good spirits and I think his experience has not injured him in any way.

There are limits to the things which may (or may not) be done in places of this kind, but I believe your son left us without any bitterness in his heart.

I have shown your letter to Mrs Smith.

With kind regards to Lady Home and to you.

I remain,
Yours sincerely,
W. SMITH

The Rt. Hon. The Earl of Home, K.T., T.D.,
The Hirsel,
Coldstream.